Cardiff's Electric Tramways

by
David Gould

THE OAKWOOD PRESS

First Edition published 1975
Second Edition 1996

British Library Cataloguing in Publication Data
A Record for this book is available from the British Library
ISBN 0 85361 487 3

Typeset by Oakwood Graphics.
Repro by Ford Graphics, Ringwood, Hants.
Printed by Alpha Print (Oxford) Ltd, Witney, Oxon.

Car No. 69 in Castle Street about to turn into High Street while working the Canton to Pier Head service. A horse bus is in the foreground, and the Marquess of Bute's vines are well in evidence on the castle wall. *Martin J. Ridley No. 7730*

Published by
The Oakwood Press
P.O. Box 122, Headington, Oxford OX3 8LU

Contents

Foreword

It may seem strange that someone who is too young to have any real recollection of Cardiff's electric tramcars, and who has not lived in the city since 1953, should have written a history of its former tramway system. Nevertheless I started gathering information on the tramways in 1963, slowly at first but with increasing momentum; fortunately it was possible to visit Cardiff at fairly frequent intervals, though the necessity of photographing the trolley buses in their last years rather held up the process of research into the tramways.

One former tram-driver, who was traffic-regulator at Gabalfa trolley bus terminus when I met him in July 1964, proved to have an excellent memory. I learnt some fascinating snippets of information, such as the location of the various single-track sections, one of which (Heathfield Road to Maitland Street) had trolley-actuated signal lights; the location of some trolley-reversers (Splott; Sneyd Street-the old Cathedral Road terminus; and Clive Street); the fact that workmen's cars were only for labourers, and white-collar workers were barred from them; and even the journey-time of certain routes. Apparently 20 minutes were allowed from Victoria Park to St Mary Street; 22 from Whitchurch Road to St Mary Street; and 32 from Cathedral Road to Clarence Road via Wood Street. Specimen fares of the 1920s were recalled: 3*d*. from Roath Park to Pier Head, 2½*d*. from Penylan Road to Pier Head, 3*d*. from Victoria Park to Pier Head, and a Workmen's Return of 3*d*. from Victoria Park to the Docks.

Ten years later, in April 1974, Mr Peter Arch of Rumney, in charge of the paint shop at Roath Depot, was of very great assistance when, from memory, he gave me the painting specification for tramcars in the 'thirties, which will be found in the chapter on livery; I have used his exact terminology. He gave me certain other information, particularly details of the tramcars.

However, most of what is in this book has come from the printed word, in particular the Cardiff City Council Minutes, issues of the *South Wales Echo* from 1902 to 1905, the *Western Mail* for May 1926 and February 1950, and a photocopy of the 1905 Tramways Rule-book, all of which were in the care of the Central Library, Working Street, Cardiff. Reference has been made to *Tramway & Railway World*, particularly the issues for 12th June, 1902, 15th April, 1915, 14th October, 1920, and 19th April, 1923; and later *Transport World*, issues for 8th July, 1943 and 12th August, 1948. Of very great value is Mr H.B. Priestley's series of articles on Cardiff tramways in the June, July, and August 1940 issues of *The Modern Tramway*; details of car numbering and introduction of routes have been taken from this. There is also an interesting article on Service No. 9, by the same author, in the July 1963 issue of *Trams*.

A superb series of articles entitled 'Cardiff's Electric Tramways', by H.B. Priestley, appeared in *Tramway Review* Nos. 84 to 93 (1975-78).

Apart from the gentlemen mentioned above, I should also like to thank Mr John H. Price for his help, particularly for the loan of innumerable newspaper cuttings and the *Guide to Cardiff & District*, William Lewis, Cardiff, *c*. 1931; and Mr Ian L. Wright for information about the water car, and details of the latter years of the tramways.

I am greatly indebted to Mr John C. Gillham for having read through this revised edition with great care, for making many recommendations for improvements, and for supplying details of several Acts of Parliament (which I

have incorporated).

My reasons for writing this history are a wish to chronicle the life of an excellent transport system, a great liking for tramways generally, and a strong affection for the city of my childhood.

Close view of the top-deck front end of a Brush-built car at Newport Road in 1947. This is a depot working; Service 5A ran between Victoria Park and St Mary Street at this time.
Ian L. Wright

Car No. 2 posed at the south-east end of Clarence Bridge (opened in 1890). The conductor and many of the local children have ensured themselves a place in the picture, but the driver - at the far end of the tram - was not so fortunate. *Martin J. Ridley No. 7736*

Car No. 5 in Queen Street travelling from Pier Head to Newport Road (Broadway) and passing Car No. 36 on its way to Pier Head. *Author's Collection*

Chapter One

Takeover of the Provincial Tramways Co. and Construction of Electric Tramways

The Welsh capital city of Cardiff, the name of which is the Anglicised form of Caer-Dyf - 'Stronghold on the Taff' - has grown at a phenomenal rate since the start of the nineteenth century. In 1801 its population was a mere 1,870; by 1891 it had increased to 129,000; and in 1981 to 279,800. The modern Welsh form of the city's name is Caerdydd.

The old town owed its prosperity to coal; to carry it down from the valleys the 25-mile Glamorganshire Canal was opened in 1798 from Merthyr to Cardiff. This soon proved inadequate, but the Taff Vale Railway Company's line from Merthyr to Cardiff, opened in 1841, and the construction two years earlier of Cardiff's first dock, the latter financed by the Second Marquess of Bute, soon allowed Cardiff to become the greatest coal-exporting port in the world, 10½ million tons passing through in the peak year of 1913.

In the late 19th century two companies ran horse-tramway services in Cardiff. The Cardiff Tramways Company, a subsidiary of the Provincial Tramways Co., was the larger of the two, with 6 miles 25 chains of route ; the other undertaking, the Cardiff District & Penarth Harbour Tramway Company, owned a line 2 miles 33 chains long.

The Cardiff Tramways Co. opened its first route from High Street to the Docks via Bute Street in 1872 and a second route north and eastwards along The Hayes, St John Square, Queen Street and Newport Road to the Royal Infirmary later that year, extending the line along Newport Road to Broadway, Roath, in 1878. A westward extension of the Docks service came about earlier in 1878, when the line was opened from High Street, along Castle Street and Cowbridge Road to Clive Road, Canton. The last horse-tram route to be opened ran from St John's Square to Cathays via Salisbury Road and began operation in December 1886. The solitary route owned by the Cardiff District & Penarth Harbour company ran from Grangetown (Ferry Road) in the south, along Penarth Road and Bute Terrace eastwards to Adamsdown (Clifton Street) and was opened in 1881.

Neither of these companies electrified its lines, fearing compulsory purchase by Cardiff Corporation who would reap the benefits of electrification at the companies expense, under Section 43 of the 1870 Tramways Act, which stated that local authorities could compulsorily purchase company-owned tramways (though not the companies themselves) after 21 years from the passing of the Act authorising their construction.

The four main tram routes, as running in the late 1890s shortly before their inevitable takeover, will now be described in detail to help the stranger to Cardiff gain some impression of the area then served; descriptions are mainly from the Guide to Cardiff published by the Ancient Order of Foresters in 1899. (N.B.: Bute Street was frequently referred to as Bute Road for many years by Cardiff people.)

Roath and Bute Docks service. Cars on this route were painted green.

Boarding the Roath car at St John's Square, we pass along the busy thoroughfare of Queen Street, having to our left the Empire Music Hall, the Park Hall and Park Place, and to the right the Taff Vale Railway station. The car now runs under the Taff Vale and Rhymney Railway bridges, after which we enter Newport Road and pass on the left the Rhymney station, the University College and Roath Wesleyan Chapel, and on the right Howard Gardens and St James' Church; further on, upon the same side, the Infirmary, and on the left Roath Court. The Newport Road terminus is at Broadway, which is seen coming in on the right.

Returning to St John's Square we stay on the car as it runs through to the Docks. We pass St John's Church and the Free Library on the right, and run through The Hayes, where there is the John Batchelor statue and an open market, and further on the Royal Arcade and the old Welsh Baptist *Tabernacl* on the right. The line now makes a sharp descent and passes under the Great Western Railway bridge, so low that passengers are earnestly warned by word of mouth and printed notices to keep their seats, and then a steep rise to the bridge over the water connecting the Glamorganshire Canal to the West Dock. The remainder of the run is through the lengthy Bute Road, where there is a bewildering variety of mercantile and consular offices, seamen's boarding houses and shops. Further down, on the left, are the Docks' post office and Board of Trade offices; on the right James Street, which leads to Clarence Bridge and Grangetown. The Merchants' Exchange is now passed, and the line terminates at the pier head, whence the steam packet *Marchioness* starts daily for Bristol and in the season numerous steamboats ply to Weston, Clevedon and Ilfracombe.

Canton and Bute Docks service. Cars on this route were painted red. Leaving the Docks and riding up Bute Road, we turn off to the left at Hayes Bridge. The car now sweeps round into the principal Cardiff thoroughfare, the busy St Mary Street, where the eye will rest on the imposing frontage of the Western Mail buildings. On the left, as the car turns, is the Bute Monument and streets leading to Grangetown and the Great Western station respectively. As the car passes up St Mary Street, on the left will be seen Wood Street and the Royal Hotel. Further up St Mary Street are the Royal and Central Arcades on the right, and on the left the Queen's Hotel, with Howell's great drapery premises opposite. On the left we now have the Town Hall and the old post office, and a little further, on the right, a peep of the beautiful tower of St John's Church.

Passing now through High Street, and leaving the Castle and High Street Arcades on the left and right respectively, we sweep round to the left into Castle Street, having on one side the Angel Hotel and on the other the Castle. Further on upon the left is the Cardiff Arms Park and on the right the Castle grounds. The rails now cross Cardiff Bridge, from which a charming view may be obtained of the River Taff. We are now in the Riverside and Canton sections of the town, with Sophia Gardens to the right, after which we pass the entrance to Cathedral Road. Following Cowbridge Road, the tram passes the Workhouse and county police station, and after a longish run lands its passengers within very easy walking distance of the pretty Victoria Park.

St John's Square and Cathays service. Cars on this route were painted yellow.

The Cathays tram follows the same route as the Roath tram through Queen Street to Windsor Place, then passes the Presbyterian and St Andrew's Churches to the right, and so under the Taff Vale Railway bridge to Salisbury Road, along Wyeverne Road and right into Woodville Road to Crwys Road, this being the nearest tramcar approach to the cemetery in Allensbank Road, the Barracks in Whitchurch Road, and Roath Park.

Grangetown and Adamsdown service. Cars on this route were painted chocolate. Leaving the western terminus at Ferry Road, Grangetown, we ride up Clive Street and turn right into Penarth Road, cross Taff Bridge and pass under two low railway bridges owned by the Great Western Railway; continue eastwards along Custom House Street, Bute Terrace (with Bute Road to our right), Adam Street, Moira Place and Constellation Street in Adamsdown, the terminus being near Roath Dock and Dowlais Iron Works and the other industries that cluster on the once solitary East Moors.

On 25th July, 1898, Cardiff Corporation obtained an Act of Parliament, 61 & 62 Vic., c.128, giving it powers to purchase, electrify and work the horse tramways; to build 8 miles 37 chains of new extensions ; also to borrow £160,000 for track reconstruction and £30,000 for land to build a power station and car depots. The new tramways authorised by the 1898 Act were:

- No. 1 2 miles 15.35 chains, from Harrowby Street along Clarence Road, Clarence Bridge, Corporation Road, Clare Road, Clare Street, Lower Cathedral Road and Cathedral Road as far as Berthwin Street.
- No. 2 16.80 chains, along Neville Street from Clare Street to Cowbridge Road.
- No. 3 35.05 chains, from Clare Street along Tudor Street and Wood Street as far as Great Western Lane.
- No. 4 1.10 chains, a curve from Clare Road into Tudor Street.
- No. 5 77.40 chains, from Queen Street along Park Place and Colum Road to North Road.
- No. 6 21.06 chains, southwards along Portmanmoor Road (Splott) from Bridgend Street to Menelaus Street.
- No. 7 3 miles 0.70 chains, from Bridgend Street northwards along Portmanmoor Road, Walker Road, Splott Road, Pearl Street, Clifton Street, Copper Street, Star Street, Planet Street, Glossop Road, Castle Road, Albany Road, Wellfield Road and Ninian Road as far as Fairoak Road.
- No. 8 1 mile 29.80 chains, from Copper Street along the rest of Clifton Street, Broadway, Newport Road, Albany Road and Pen-y-lan Road to Ninian Road.

Nos. 1, 2, 3, 4 and 6 were to be wholly double track, whilst Nos. 5, 7 and 8 were to be mostly double track but with several short sections of single track. In fact Nos. 1-4 and 6 were constructed entirely, No. 7 partly so, but Nos. 5 and 8 never were built. (Castle Road was renamed City Road in 1905; Pen-y-lan is often rendered as Penylan.)

The estimates placed before Parliament had been based on the conduit system of electrification. Nevertheless, a year later, the Chairman of the Tramways Committee, Thomas Andrews, the deputy chairman, and the borough engineer, W. Harpur, visited various tramway systems to decide which system to use, and found in favour of the overhead trolley wire, which was adopted.

Arthur Ellis, MIME, MIEE, was appointed electrical engineer in June 1900, and in December he became the borough electrical engineer and manager of the Electric Lighting & Tramways Department. Construction of the first new route began in the same month; the borough engineer undertook to re-lay track on the routes cheaper and quicker than any of the firms that had tendered for the work.

Rails used were of the girder type, 6¼ in. deep, with 7 in. wide base, and a groove 1¼ in. wide by 1¼ in. deep; rail length was 45 ft. and weight per yard 100 lb. The first consignment of rails was supplied by Dick, Kerr & Co. Ltd; the second batch by Bolckow, Vaughan & Co. Ltd. Tie bars were specially designed by Mr Harpur. Points and crossings came from Askham Bros and Wilson Ltd and Hadfields Steel Foundry Co. Ltd. The rails were laid on a concrete bed 11 in. deep and 18 in. wide and the track was double-bonded at each joint and cross-bonded every three yards.

Tracks were paved in wood blocks of Jarrah and red gum. The wood was purchased in bulk and cut into bricks 9 in. x 3 in. x 4 in. at the Corporation sawmill. At the sides of the rails, chilled cast iron paving blocks were laid alternately with the wood blocks.

All the overhead equipment was erected by the Department; the highly artistic standards, bases and brackets were designed by Mr Ellis and made by J. Russell & Sons. The standards were erected in the centre of the road wherever possible. A site in Newport Road, Roath, was acquired and a power station of 3,000 kw capacity was under construction, and a depot to hold a hundred cars was being built nearby. This was opened on 18th September, 1902. The Tramway Offices were in The Hayes. A smaller depot was also opened in Clare Road on the opposite side of the town.

The first portion of new tramway was opened with a service of horse cars in June 1901; and on 1st January, 1902, the Corporation took possession from midnight of the main Cardiff company's 52 cars and 342 horses, and all lines of route except a horse-bus route from Cardiff to Whitchurch, and began to work them. £50,000 was paid to the Tramways Co. for their lines, and £15,644 for the cars and horses. Most of the local employees of the company were taken over, and more would be needed in the future. The changeover was effected smoothly; it was not obvious to the casual observer that the tramways were being worked by new owners. The Adamsdown-Grangetown line of the other company stayed independent, for the time being.

Work of renewing the lines for electrification had begun in Queen Street. The Tramways Committee decided that the traction poles should be placed along the centre of St Mary Street, High Street and Queen Street, as, apart from possible objections from tradespeople, it was difficult to erect poles on the 'side walks' because of the presence of a great many pipes.

The new route from Cathedral Road to the Docks (Clarence Road) was expected to be opened with a service of horse cars on the 10th January.

Delivery of new electric tramcars began; they arrived by railway, over the Taff Vale's Roath branch (with top deck fittings removed) and were unloaded over a temporary length of track run from a siding into Newport Road and the Roath Depot.

On 25th March, 1902, the first electric tramcar in Cardiff's streets was driven by Arthur Ellis. 'Members assembled at St John's Square and left that point in horse cars, proceeding to the Tramway Power Station, where they inspected the premises and machinery therein. They returned to St John's Square in an Electric Car, the engineer and Manager acting as driver thereof.'

Major R. E. Druitt, R.E., and Inspector A.P. Trotter of the Board of Trade officially inspected the tramways on 22nd April. They left the Angel Hotel at 9.30 am, boarding car No. 1 at Wood Street, being joined by the borough engineer, W. Harpur; C.E. Davies, Ellis's chief assistant; and other Corporation officials. Mr Ellis was absent through illness. A second car, No. 2, contained Councillors Thomas Andrews and John Courtis, chairman and vice-chairman respectively of the Tramways Committee; and other members. Says the *South Wales Echo* of the occasion: 'The weather was at first boisterous, rain falling in drenching showers, but subsequently the sky cleared, and the inspectors and the company were able to travel on the outside of the cars.'

The inspectors toured Tudor Street, Neville Street and Cowbridge Road to the Canton terminus, then back again and via Clare Road to the Docks. They spent some time examining the wiring over Clarence Bridge, which was opened and closed several times at the inspectors' request. They suggested that an automatic cut-out should be provided there, in order that current be cut off for a short distance either side of the bridge while it was open. The centre span of this bridge over the Taff River - which had been inaugurated on 17th September, 1890, by the Duke of Clarence and Avondale - could be swung through 90 degrees, and four men could operate it in five minutes.

From Clarence Bridge the ensemble travelled to the Cathedral Road terminus and back to Wood Street; then over new track in Mill Lane to St. John's Square; to Roath Park via Castle Road, then the Newport Road line and so to the Power Station. 'Here the inspectors were heard expressing their gratification with the excellent quality of the work done.'

The inspection finished shortly after 1.00 pm; according to the *South Wales Echo* it had covered six route miles and ten track miles. The inspectors, who were well satisfied with both track and wiring, promised to issue a certificate authorising public opening.

Three days later, at a Tramways Committee meeting, the Chairman stated that electric cars would run from Newport Road (Broadway) to the Docks via Wood Street and Clare Road until the Bute Road route was completed.

Alderman Jacobs suggested: 'Can't you run the workmen's car right through?'

'We are doing that from this morning,' replied Mr Ellis. 'We are very hard-up for cars. Every available horse car is in use.'

Mr John Jenkins asked, 'What is the contract in regard to the supply of cars?'

Mr Ellis said that Messrs Dick, Kerr of Preston were very much behind in deliveries, but they had promised to deliver ten cars a week. In a fortnight 37 cars would be ready for service.

Plans for future extensions included: Constellation Street-Meteor Street-Infirmary to Castle Road; Moira Terrace to Adam Street; Fitzalan Road, connecting Queen Street with Moira Place and Splott; an extension of the

Cowbridge Road route to Victoria Park; Ninian Road to Roath Park Lake; Cathedral Road to Llandaff Fields; and Castle Road to Whitchurch Road Barracks. Most of these were eventually completed, but Fitzalan Road never saw trams. As previously noted, Castle Road was the old name for City Road, so renamed in 1905, and should not be confused with Castle Street; it took its name from the long-vanished Roath Castle (Plas Newydd). On 28th April, 1902, the Board of Trade sanction was dispatched, and two days later a Certificate authorising public use of the tramways that had been inspected on the 22nd was received by Cardiff's Town Clerk. It was feared that on the opening day there would be traffic congestion in some places, and the general manager suggested that the horse car service be suspended for a couple of hours. He also submitted a revised timetable, which was adopted. Eighteen new electric trams were to be used, twelve on the Castle Road-Wood Street-Clarence Road (Docks) line; and six on the Roath line, Newport Road (Broadway) to the Monument. The General Manager aimed at having a 5-minute service on the Castle Road section from the corner of Penylan and Wellfield Roads; a 20-minute service to Roath Park terminus; and a five-minute service on the Roath(Newport Road) line.

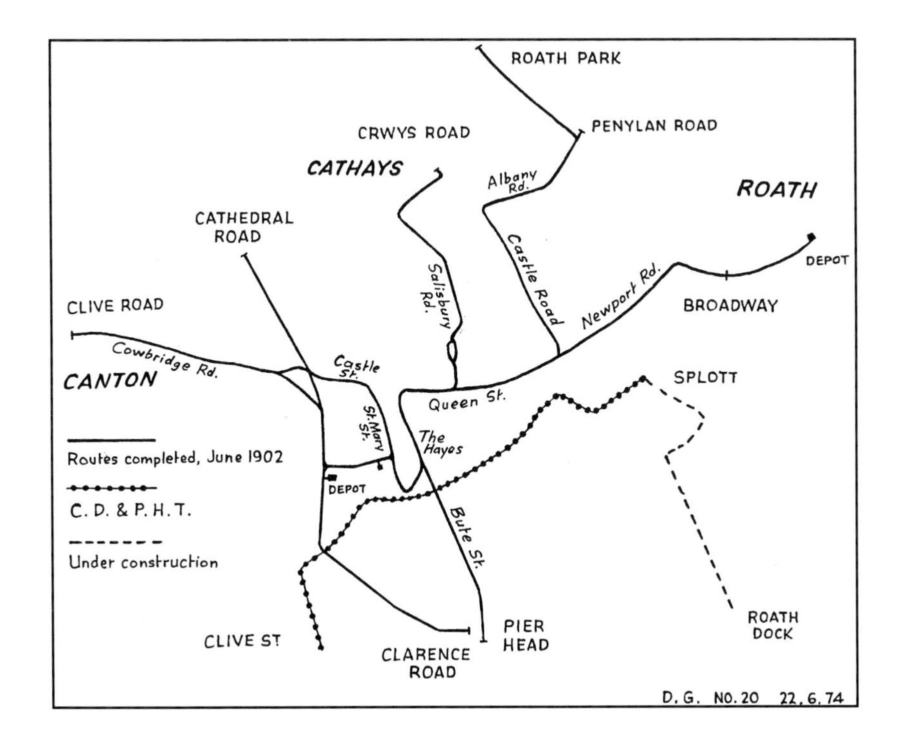

Chapter Two

The Opening

Although only twenty electric trams had been delivered, all the routes which had been constructed were formally opened on Thursday, 1st May, 1902. Ceremonial trips were attended by a large party invited by the Mayor, Councillor F.J. Beavan, J.P. Twelve gaily bedecked cars were assembled outside the Town Hall, in St Mary Street, and the Mayor drove tramcar No. 1 to Canton, Cathedral Road and Clarence Road, followed by a procession of the other eleven cars. The chairman of the Tramways Committee then drove the party to Newport Road, and the Deputy Chairman drove along Castle Road. There was one minor derailment, otherwise the whole ceremony went very smoothly. There was a sense of wonder at this new mechanical transport, which was regarded as a great stride forward.

After the ceremony there was luncheon at the Town Hall. Electric cars ran a service on the Roath (Broadway) and Penylan Road routes to Town until 8 pm and twelve to twenty cars ran on those routes from 7.30 am next day. The other services had to continue being worked by horse cars until further electric cars were delivered.

Naturally enough, the new installation suffered from minor defects: only two days after the opening the *South Wales Echo* reported:

> This afternoon the new electric trams at Cardiff came to a stop owing to a breakdown at the Roath Power Station, the precise nature of which has not been divulged. All that the public knows is that the cars came to a sudden stoppage when the propelling agency gave out, and there they stuck. After about a couple of hours the defect was partly, or wholly, remedied, and the cars began to run again.

There was a tremendous amount of wrangling over the proposal to run a Sunday tram service; several Conservative and Liberal clubs, representing 4,000 members, had protested. It was moved that no employee of the tramways department should be allowed to work more than six days, 8½ hours a day, in each week. Thomas Andrews proposed that tramwaymen's hours a week should be 54, with time and a half for Sundays, although any man with a conscientious objection should not be expected to work. It was decided that Sunday services should start at 2 pm and finish at 10 pm.

Almost at once, a deputation against the Sunday running proposals arrived from the Free Churches, representing 20,000 worshippers. Cardiff County Council also discussed a petition from combined political clubs. Hard things were said; the Mayor was firmly against Sunday running.

It was argued that the 4,000 Liberals and Conservatives were nothing compared with 24,000 Cardiff ratepayers, and running Sunday services would be the right and proper thing in the interests of the majority. It would also be in the Tramway Committee's own interests, as the absence of a Sunday service would be a gift of one day a week to the bus company.

Eventually, a resolution in favour of Sunday trams was carried by 20 votes to 13.

By the 9th May, of the 54 electric cars ordered, 26 were in service. A tender from Dick, Kerr for a supply of 40 more was accepted, prices being £650 each for bogie double-deck cars (Nos. 75-94) and £540 for four wheelers (Nos. 55-74).

Electric cars started running on the Canton (Clive Road)-Neville Street-Wood Street-Town route and from Roath Park to Town from 13th May, using five and three cars respectively. The Bute Road route was completed six and a half weeks early; the last wood block for the relaid tramway track was laid on the morning of Saturday 17th May, 1902. The completion date had been set at 1st July. From the following Monday, a temporary service of horse cars ran along Bute Road from The Hayes to Pier Head.

Sunday services between Roath and Town, and Canton, Wood Street, and Roath Park, using five and twelve cars respectively, began on 25th May. The latter service, re-routed via Castle Street and High Street, was made daily from 20th June.

The first recorded accident involving the electric tramway occurred on the evening of 26th May, 1902, when Mr Elias Light was cycling along Queen Street towards Town. He was at the rear of a tram, but tried to pass it on the *right* within thirty yards of Windsor Place. A tram going to Roath, driven by Alfred James, came up, and Light crashed into it, and was thrown against the car going to town. One of its wheels passed over his left hand, which later had to be amputated at the Infirmary. He subsequently applied for compensation but failed to get it. As Mr Ellis pointed out, the accident was Light's own fault as he should have kept to the correct side of the road.

Electric cars started running from Cathedral Road via Lower Cathedral Road to Clarence Road from 30th May. There was a ten-minute service between 8 am and 11.30 pm, using four cars. New services began between Roath and Pier Head, replacing the Roath-Monument service, and between Cathays and the Monument on 13th June. Ten and six trams respectively were required. The Roath Park-Monument service was withdrawn on 19th June, 1902; electric cars were introduced to the Cathedral Road-St Mary Street-Clarence Road service on 20th June. The Penylan Road-Town service was extended to Pier Head on 13th June.

There was still considerable delay in delivery of new electric tramcars. In July Thomas Andrews, the Chairman, declared that it caused them a great loss, especially on busy days. They still did not have enough cars to go round. The Town Clerk was instructed to write to Dick, Kerr & Co. Ltd demanding immediate delivery. It is almost certain that the manufacturers were working at great pressure as it was, but this does not seem to have occurred to the Chairman. The Committee, in the meantime, resolved to obtain a single-deck car for trial, at a cost of £600, with a smoking compartment; and also a number of dry-seats.

The General Manager wanted to know if the Taff Vale Railway took precedence over the tramway at Bute Street level-crossing, to which query Councillor Roberts answered 'They have always exercised the right to be first.' It was decided to see Mr H. Riches, the TVR locomotive superintendent, about the question.

Many tram-horses had been sold off at about £17 17*s*. a head, realising £1,608, regarded as a very good price.

Councillor Crossman said he had been asked by the Trades Council to suggest that workmen's cars be run between Canton and Roath (Broadway) at 5.30 in the morning and 5.15 in the evening. Mr Ellis answered that the introduction of horse cars interfered with the service, but he hoped that electric workmen's cars would start in a month.

Mr Ellis said that the tramcar life-guard, two of which were required to be carried by every car, one at each end, had been put to the test on the 8th July, for that evening in Bute Street a drunken woman walked in front of a tram, which knocked her down. However she got up and ran away before the driver could get down. She was thoroughly drunk, but Mr Ellis was confident that the shock had sobered her.

'That's a new cure for drunkenness,' remarked the Chairman.

The Mayor, F.J. Beavan, replied, 'I shall recommend it to the magistrates.'

A service began on 11th July between Clive Road, Neville Street and Clarence Road, requiring four trams to work it. Three days later, 121 more horses from Severn Road depot were sold by auction at Cathays tramway depot: 98 were described as 'aged' - over nine years old. Prices varied from 2½, to 36 guineas, averaging about 13 guineas each.

Receipts for the three months ending 30th June were £15,484 6*s*. 4*d*. - an increase of £8,276 19s. 4*d*. over the previous quarter. The average receipts from each car per day were £3 11*s*. 5*d*., an increase of £1. 3,696,123 passengers were carried, which was 1,966,355 more than the previous quarter. Doubtless much of this general increase was due to electrification; indeed the future looked rosy. About this time Mr Ellis had an offer from Lisbon Tramways to act as manager, but he did not accept as he was under contract to stay at Cardiff for five years. Actually he was to stay with Cardiff Corporation until 1920.

On 26th July the last horse cars ran between Clive Road and Town. Two days later there was a sale of horse cars held in Severn Road, although it had been originally advertised to be held in the Wood Street depot. Perhaps because of this the attendance was poor, and only five cars were sold, at £8 each. There were still 16 in use, and 30 more to be sold off.

On 8th August, 1902, a new 'Circular' route began operating between Clive Road (Canton) and Town, using six cars; it was not really circular, but ran via Neville Street, Wood Street, High Street and Castle Street, alternate cars travelling in the opposite direction via Castle Street, High Street, Wood Street and Neville Street, thence Cowbridge Road in both directions.

The electrical engineer submitted plans for street lighting from the traction poles, replacing the pillars in existence for the lighting. A decision was made to light Cowbridge Road up to the Clive Road terminus, as well as St Mary Street and Bute Road as far as Pier Head; Newport Road; Albany Road and Wellfield road, as far as Roath Park entrance; Castle Road and Queen Street. £500 from the tramway profits would be set aside for a reserve fund.

There was a certain amount of criticism levelled at the Corporation for employing men living outside Cardiff on the tramways. The Chairman dryly commented that if they carried the cry of Cardiff work for Cardiff men as far as

some members wanted, they might ask themselves where they would be if Wales for the Welsh had been observed. The General Manager did not think there were more than fifteen men from outside the borough working on the cars.

Further services were introduced, presumably as fresh cars arrived: Roath Park and Pier Head (Sundays only), using six cars, from the 17th August, and Cathays to Pier Head from 5th September, using three, but this was withdrawn in May 1903.

An alarming incident occurred on the afternoon of 11th September, 1902. The heavy covering of a section box in Cowbridge Road flew out with a loud report; no one was hurt. The paint on the traction pole caught fire and, as the smoke was coming from the joint between the base and the pole, it appeared that the underground insulation was on fire. It was believed that a short circuit had occurred owing to rain water leaking through, and the fuse did not blow as it should have done. Traffic was delayed on this section for almost an hour while, under Mr Ellis's direction, skilled workmen repaired the damage sufficiently to allow traffic to be resumed.

On the 19th September, the *South Wales Echo* reported that time recorders were being put up at various points on the tramway system:

> To the uninitiated they appear to be nothing more than an ordinary clock, in a stained case, but in addition to serving the useful purpose of denoting the time to the public, they act as a check on drivers and conductors, the last-named having at the end of each journey to apply a key to a certain piece of mechanism, and this indicates how long it has taken to travel to and from the various points.

By 1905 the locations of these Bundy recording clocks were: Clive Road, Canton; Cathedral Road, just short of the terminus; Clarence Bridge; Clive Street, Grangetown; Bute Street, near the station; Aberdovey Street, Splott; Roath Court; Wellfield Road; and Crwys Road junction.

From 3rd October, 1902, the workmen's service of horse cars was withdrawn, being replaced by electric cars; it was feared that workmen would soil the new trams, as a notice was inserted that 'the management invites the assistance of artisan passengers in maintaining the cars in a clean and serviceable condition, and trust that no passenger will smoke inside, or spit in or on the cars, as it is necessary that the cars shall be kept running during the busy period of the morning for general traffic.' Workmen could travel any distance for 1*d*.

The last horse trams ran on 17th October, 1902; the electric tram was now the sole means of municipal transport.

The Board of Trade issued a circular in January 1903 stating that every electric car should be fitted with a speed indicator within six months, and at night should display a white light in front and a red one at the rear. At a BoT conference in London it had been suggested that the regulation speed be 7½ mph, including stops; but the BoT could not agree. The BoT inspector had jocularly stated,

> With the white light only the driver of any vehicle running in the same direction or overtaking the car might take the car for the shop window and run into it - and with the

red light, any man in charge of an overtaking vehicle would know that unless it was a chemist's shop it would be an electric car.

As Cardiff tramcars were using a complicated arrangement of discs, crosses, and lights at night to indicate the route, this new regulation would ruin the system, and the cars would have to be rewired. The Town Clerk was therefore instructed to state to the Board of Trade the Council's objection.

In February 1903 tenders were considered from seven firms for twenty 4-wheel double-deck cars; that of the British Thomson-Houston Co. was accepted, at £504 per car, a total of £10,080. They would be similar to those already running, and became Nos. 95-114. Mr Ellis was instructed to secure a price from BTH for one single-deck *combination* bogie car 36 feet long with seats for 18 smokers. There would be no screens at either end. This car was duly ordered, built by G.F. Milnes & Co., and upon delivery became No. 115.

Bogie car No. 25 turns into Mill Lane from St Mary Street while working the Clive Road to Roath Park service. The lines in the foreground turn into Custom House Street and are connected to the lines leading (*left*) to Penarth Road. *Raphael Tuck & Sons*

Single-deck car No. 47 at the St Mary Street terminus of the Cathays (Crwys Road) via Salisbury Road route; also in view is a line of five horse-cabs. *Frederick Hartmann No. 2525/6*

Car No. 38 at the Pier Head terminus, Bute Street, looking north. Centre background is Bute Road station, Taff Vale Railway. *Ernest T. Bush No. 2238*

Chapter Three

Takeover and Reconstruction of the CD&PH Tramway

It will be recalled that Cardiff Corporation had not taken over the Cardiff District & Penarth Harbour Tramway Company's Adamsdown-Grangetown line in January 1902, but nevertheless it wished to do so. Agreement of the purchase price took some time to come to, however.

The line was not a gold-mine: the Tramways Committee recommended that the horse-car service to Splott, i.e. the far end of the Adamsdown area, should cease as soon as possible, the horses being sold. The cars were losing £500 a month, taking about 2½*d*. per car per mile. Transfer tickets were, it seemed, very troublesome, and encouraged swindling. The line was owned by the CD&PH company but from January 1896 it had been leased to the Provincial Tramways Co. Ltd for 21 years.

Negotiations between the Cardiff Corporation Tramways Committee and the CD&PH Tramway Company ended in January 1903. The Corporation had originally offered £10,000 to take over the company, who had asked for £18,000, later reducing it to £13,000; however, the Corporation did not care to pay that amount, but rather than have the matter settled by arbitration, continued to try to make terms. At a conference on 2nd January, Corporation representatives advanced their offer to £11,500, and the company Directors reduced their claim to £12,500. Deadlock was reached, but eventually they decided to split the difference and the final figure decided upon was £12,000.

The takeover (from noon on 10th February, 1903) enabled the Corporation to start work on electrifying the line in Custom House Street in order to link up St Mary Street to Bute Street by new junctions. It was also planned to reconstruct and electrify the whole line from Splott to Grangetown.

On Wednesday 11th February, 1903, work started early in the morning on relaying the track in Custom House Street. Additionally a start was made on renewing iron girders in Custom House Bridge, which carried the street over the Glamorganshire Canal. Mr Harpur, the borough engineer, expected that the junctions between the bottom of St Mary Street and Custom House Street and also Bute Street would be completed in six weeks. The intention was to run cars from Canton via Cardiff Bridge, St Mary Street and Bute Street to the Docks.

On the same date, work began on relaying track in Adamsdown, along Tin Street and Constellation Street, and by 27th February the programme was well advanced; track was laid in Tin Street between Clifton Street and Metal Street, and the ground prepared as far as System Street.

On Wednesday, 25th March, 1903, John Wesley Courtis, now Chairman of the Tramways Committee, formally opened the new tramway service from Canton to Pier Head via Custom House Street. That this was considered an important event was evidenced by the fact that Committee members went in a special car over the new section. Meanwhile, tramway track works started at the south end of Clive Street, Grangetown. Regular service between Canton (Clive Road) and Pier Head began on 26th March.

Electric services between Bute Terrace and Splott started on 20th May, 1903; six cars were needed to operate them. Thus the eastern side of the old CD&PH line was operational, but the western half, along Penarth Road and Clive Street to Grangetown, was not - and nearly never was, for at a meeting of the Cardiff Corporation on 5th August, 1903, Sir Thomas Morel, a leading citizen and commercial man, moved that the resolution empowering reconstruction of this line be rescinded, as the Corporation was now in a bad way financially. Councillor Courtis agreed that it would be an 'extravagant waste of public money,' and in any case there would be no cars to work the line. Cardiff had been £3,000,000 in debt in March and was even more so in August. Even so, said Councillor F.J. Beavan, the work of reconstruction was necessary and would not cost so very much.

Later in the month, a question was raised concerning doubling the Penarth Road line between Taff Bridge and the corner of Corporation Road. The Corporation had power to re-lay and use a single line only, but wished to lay double track. Lord Bute and Lord Windsor owned that part of the road and when assent was sought it was not, unfortunately, forthcoming. It was not until 1921 that this section was doubled.

Construction of the line between Corporation Road and the Great Western Railway bridge was completed in the first week of December 1903. It was realised that more single-deck cars would have to be ordered, otherwise it would be difficult to handle the traffic which the following summer would bring. A number of double-deck cars had been stripped for conversion into single-deck ones. The combination car, previously mentioned, had not proved successful and, although Mr Ellis felt the best plan would be to advertise for single-deck cars of the same type as those already running, on 15th December, 1903, the Committee accepted the tender of the British Westinghouse Company for the supply of 15 single-deck combination cars. The cost was to be £601 10s. each, and the cars, which would accommodate 40 seated passengers, including 10 smokers, would be open-ended (Nos. 116-130).

The new line to Grangetown via Penarth Road was ready for traffic in January 1904 and, after its BoT inspection, was opened on 9th February, through services running between Clive Street (Grangetown) and Splott via Penarth Road, Custom House Street, Bute Terrace and Adamsdown. Until then, a temporary service between Bute Terrace and Clive Street via Wood Street and Clare Road had been running since 27th June, 1903.

Chapter Four

Consolidation of Routes and Services

The Splott-Grangetown tramway was never a money-spinner, and the fact that it had to be worked by single-deck cars because of the presence of three low railway bridges was always a disadvantage. Although connected to the main system at five points, the line always appeared to be run separately from the other routes, as though it were still independent. The single-deck cars were unpopular with some passengers, for on the Salisbury Road line, where also they were used owing to the low railway bridge preventing the passage of double-deck cars, we find one greengrocer claiming that in hot weather the single-deck cars were 'regular cucumber houses'. Thus, in July 1903, a deputation of ratepayers in the Cathays area sought to persuade the Council to lower the road under the Salisbury Road bridge in order that double-deck cars might be run. The deputation underestimated the cost (£4,000) because they had reckoned on a 15 feet headroom, whereas the Board of Trade would, it was stated, insist on 16 feet: so nothing was done.

On 17th July, 1903, heavy rainfall caused flooding up to three feet under Salisbury Road bridge, while in Newport Road there were no trams for a quarter of an hour because of floods up to two or three feet under the Taff Vale Railway bridge in Queen Street.

On Wednesday, 2nd September, Agnes Gilchrist appeared at Cardiff Police Court for the eightieth time! She had thrown herself on the tram track just as the car was approaching. She said, 'It is my own fault; I got a drop of drink.' She was given a fortnight's imprisonment, to the great relief, probably, of the motorman of the tram concerned.

An incident that upset the smooth-running of the tramway occurred on 5th September, 1903, on the Canton section. The trolley of a tramcar travelling from Clive Road became dewired and, springing up, struck a feeder in the centre, bending it appreciably. This caused the feeder, and the wires adjacent to it, to droop. Cars from Clive Road to Town had to travel via Neville Street, although services from Town were able to use the normal routing, owing to a dip in the road at the point of the incident, enabling them to coast on the favourable grade past the portion of wiring affected by the accident. The trolley feeder was removed and the defect remedied

Another Act of Parliament was obtained on 11th August, 1903, as 3 Edw. VII, c.145, and this authorised the construction of another eight tramway extensions. Tramway No. 1 had been deleted from the Bill, whilst the eight that survived were:

No. 2 20.80 chains, along Crwys Road from Albany Road to Woodville Road.
No. 3 48.50 chains, along Crwys Road and Whitchurch Road from Woodville Road to Talygarn Street.
No. 4 13.97 chains, along Meteor Street from Constellation Street to Planet Street.
No. 5 12.50 chains, along Moira Terrace from Moira Place to Meteor Street.

Car No. 11 on the Bute Terrace to Grangetown via Wood Street and Clare Road service poses with its crew in Clive Street, Grangetown, probably around 1904. *D.W.K. Jones Collection*

Car No. 37 in Newport Road travelling to Town one sunny morning about 1905. The conductor on the rear platform and all the bowler-hatted passengers on the top deck are turning round to gaze at the photographer. *J. Valentine No. 39444*

No. 6 18.87 chains, along Fitzalan Road from Newport Road to Moira Place.
No. 7 9.70 chains, along Cathedral Road from Berthwin Street to the Borough boundary.
No. 8 59.45 chains, along Cowbridge Road from Clive Road to Aldsworth Road and then turning into Aldsworth Road for about five chains.
No. 9 60.30 chains, from Adam Street along Windsor Road, Sanquhar Street and Ordell Street to join the Splott tramway in Portmanmoor Road.

These eight authorised lines came to a total of 3 miles 3.79 chains. Nos. 2, 3, 5, 6 and 7 were to be wholly double track; No. 8 was to be double line except for the last 13.95 chains at the outer end; and Nos. 4 and 9 were to be all single track except for passing loops at one and six (respectively) specified places. What actually happened was that Nos. 2, 3 and 4 were soon constructed, Nos. 5 and 7 were constructed years later, No. 8 was built only as far as Victoria Park Road West, and Nos. 6 and 9 were never built.

Cardiff Council decided on 14th September, 1903, to extend the tramway from the top of Castle Road, along Crwys Road and Whitchurch Road to a terminus opposite Talygarn Street. This extension was very necessary, as it would provide a much-needed service to residents of the upper part of Cathays, also providing an alternative route to Town worked by double-deck cars, and would avoid having to lower the road under the Salisbury Road bridge. This route would remain single-deck operated.

On 25th September, Councillor Illtyd Thomas pointed out the necessity of extending the Cowbridge Road route, as previously put forward, to Victoria Park. Councillor J.W. Courtis, the Chairman, reported that the single-track section in Castle Road, between The Parade and the junction with Newport Road, was a cause of trouble and he suggested that a sub-committee should decide what to do about the delays. The Borough Engineer felt that part of Newport Road should be widened between West Grove and the Rhymney Railway bridge at Queen Street. He said a decision had been made to construct a tramway along Glossop Road and Meteor Street, linking Newport Road with Constellation Street.

At a Tramways Committee meeting on 30th November, the Town Clerk reported that he had received a Board of Trade sanction to start work on the following tramway improvements:

1. Lay double and interlacing tracks in Mill Lane to replace single line.
2. Lay junctions between Newport Road and Glossop Road.
3. Put in a junction between Penarth Road and Mill Lane.
4. Put in a passing place in The Hayes.

In January 1904 it was agreed to go ahead with the following tramway extensions, subject to the Board of Trade's consent: along Crwys Road from Mackintosh Place to Woodville Road, to cost £2,940; along Crwys Road and Whitchurch Road from Woodville Road to Talygarn Street, to cost £6,868, and from the existing terminus on Cowbridge Road to the west side of Victoria Park, costing £4,100. Councillor Illtyd Thomas's suggestion that the Cowbridge Road extension be taken as far as the entrance to Ely Paper Mills was not adopted -

the Chairman, J.W. Courtis, stated that it would cost £2,200 for a double line. The other extensions were operationally desirable, but this one would not be justified.

Later in January the borough engineer reported that the connecting line from Constellation Street to the Royal Infirmary was completed. On 23rd April, 1904, a new service over this section began running between The Hayes (Royal Arcade) and Aberdovey Street (Splott), via Queen Street, Newport Road, Glossop Road, Meteor Street and Constellation Street, using double-deck cars.

It was agreed to construct a turning circle at Roath Park terminus; this was laid in time for the summer season, and cost £403 0*s*. 4*d*., being paid for out of revenue. As the Roath Park line was the most profitable one of the system, this expense was justified, as it meant that up to five cars could load or unload at the terminus, then leave in procession down the then single line in Ninian Road.

In March 1904, Arthur Ellis had the remarkable idea that if the Tramways Committee were willing to pay for a band to play in Roath Park during the season, at a cost of about five or six pounds a day, such an attraction could mean an increase of £50 in tramway receipts for the day. This suggestion received the blessing of the Parks Committee, and the Tramways Committee went ahead. In June of that year, Mr Ellis reported that on one day when a band was playing there were 12,000 people in the park, and on the Wednesday in Whit-week there were 49 cars running on the Roath Park route, all packed. It had cost the Tramways Committee only £50 to provide for a band in June, and Ellis urged that the committee provide for the band during July; the expenditure of a further £50 was agreed to.

However, this apparent favouritism was not taken kindly to by other areas of Cardiff; in July Councillor Richards said it appeared that the Victoria Park concerts were quite as popular as those in Roath Park, and would the Tramways Committee make a grant towards music in Victoria Park? John Courtis unsympathetically replied that if Canton people were prepared to pay a higher tram fare the Committee would consider it. Some parks, indeed, had no band at all, and in August Councillor Chappell protested that bands were placed only at points on tramway lines which had proved most profitable to the tramways. By the end of the season, the Tramways Committee had paid £115 to provide Roath Park with one extra band per week.

Although wood blocks as a road surface were cheaper than macadam— the cost of highway maintenance having decreased by £5,600 a year since their introduction six years ago - granite setts were apparently even cheaper than wood blocks. In May 1904 Crwys Road tradesmen and residents requested that wood blocks be used in Crwys Road, but Cardiff Council stated that the extra cost would be £1,032. A motion to use wood was defeated by one vote.

In July 1904, the trustees of Woodville Road Baptist Chapel objected to a proposal to double the line leading round the corner of Woodville Road, on grounds that there would be insufficient clearance between rail and kerb for vehicles to stand outside the chapel.

'And this is one of the chapels where a resolution against Sunday cars was practically unanimously carried,' said Illtyd Thomas.

'What has that to do with it?' inquired Councillor James Munn. 'The vehicles

spoken of here are for weddings and funerals.'

Members were reminded that, under the Act, no tramway could be laid within nine feet six inches of the kerb if one third of the frontagers objected. In this case, permission was sought to reduce the pavement width to give the required clearance.

In those days it was thought very uncivilised to have standing passengers in tramcars, and a new Tramways byelaw proposed that no car should contain more than the full number of passengers for whom seats were provided 'except the permission of the conductor be first obtained.' Even this qualifying phrase was objected to by one councillor as a direct encouragement to overcrowding, but nevertheless the byelaw stood.

Tramway receipts for August Bank Holiday week were a record £2,808 18*s*. 4*d*., being £212 more than the same week in 1903. The Chairman's happy comment was 'The elements had been very kind to the tramways.' Working of tramways for the year ended 31st March, 1904: Total income, £108,442; working expenses, £69,478; gross profit, £39,964; net surplus balance, £7,724; cost per car per mile 5.818*d*.; fare receipts, £101,794. Like a good General Manager, Mr Ellis gave an impartial comment:

> We are not really getting what we are entitled to receive. If you wish to see larger profits it can only be done by increasing or equalising the fares upon the various sections. If, on the other hand, the convenience of the public is considered the most important, then the results obtained cannot well be criticised. You cannot, however, have both.

During the year 23,574,204 passengers had been carried, equal to 143 times Cardiff's population, compared with 17,718,992 the previous year; cars running between Castle Road and Pier Head, and Castle Road and Canton alone earned £29,896. Various and ingenious devices were resorted to by passengers to avoid paying fares, and it seems that in this Bute Street was the worst offender. All renewals and repairs to overhead wiring and cars were paid for out of revenue. To facilitate overhead repairs, two petrol-driven tower wagons had been ordered from the South Wales Motor Co. in August, and the first of these was inspected by the Tramways Committee two months later. They were made at the Mercedes works, and were intended to replace the existing cumbersome wagons drawn by dray horses.

Some towns may have had difficulty in disposing of the hundreds of pennies collected on trams, but not Cardiff. The National & Provincial Bank took them all in; a record day's take being £80, but about £65 a day being normal. The Corporation had the task of disposing of other items too - articles left on trams by absent-minded passengers: hundreds of umbrellas, and gloves, handbags, books, an afternoon tea tray, a silver watch, four, trimmers' shovels, a roll of lead piping, a pair of pince-nez, ballroom slippers and a fine hairbrush. All were auctioned.

The extension of the Cowbridge Road tramway from Clive Road to Victoria Park was completed on 17th November, 1904; and the junction at the end of Woodville Road on the 23rd. Major Druitt of the Board of Trade inspected both extensions on the 24th November, and both were opened to traffic the same

Car No. 28 on a workmen's service in Newport Road one sunny afternoon about 1905.
Raphael Tuck & Sons

Car No. 30 at the south end of St Mary Street, caught while working the Canton-Queen Street-Roath Park service about 1905.
Author's Collection

day. A new service from Talygarn Street (Whitchurch Road) to St Mary Street via Castle Road and Queen Street began, as did a peak-hours service between Talygarn Street and Pier Head via Castle Road, also Queen Street and Bute Street. The Salisbury Road single-deck cars were also extended from the Crwys Road terminus to Talygarn Street.

The hint of increased fares was acted upon; proposals for a halfpenny rise were announced in November 1904 and took effect from 1st January, 1905. Broadway to Pier Head became 2½*d*. instead of 2*d*.; Fairoak Road to Clive Road 3½*d*. instead of 3*d*.; Penylan Road to Clive Road 3*d*. instead of 2*d*.; Clive Road to Pier Head 2½*d*. The penny stages were shortened so that passengers from Broadway could go only as far as Park Place, instead of St John's Square or The Hayes; and Penylan Road to Queen Street became 1*d*., instead of to Wood Street or The Hayes.

No town, on taking over a tramway from a company, had hitherto charged higher fares than that company; in Cardiff, a penny fare now carried a passenger 2,308 yards, compared with London, 4,400 yards, or Glasgow, 4,048 yards. Alderman Trounce said that, while the system should be put on a sound financial basis, this should be done by stopping capital charges and revenue expenses, not by fare increases. However, some towns carried their passengers even less distance for a penny: Aberdeen, for example, only 1,540 yards! In Cardiff, workmen could travel up to five miles for a penny. It was essential to put aside some money for future development, such as track renewal, due in about 13 years.

It was hoped that the low average speed of Cardiff's trams (6 mph) could be improved by eliminating several stopping places; hence 11 were abandoned and five made optional.

Early in 1905, Ellis was asked to determine whether it would be better either to start the Sunday tram service earlier in the day - so that churchgoers could use it - or else charge a fare and a half to make the existing service remunerative. The loss per car mile was 0.67*d*.; paying the men time and a half caused this loss, but there was no question of discontinuing the service, as over 27,000 people used it every Sunday. Running fewer cars in daily service had resulted in a saving, but keeping the road in repair eighteen inches either side of the tracks was a drain on expenditure, and, until the Corporation had made provision for track renewal, nothing could be given for relief of rates.

Mr Ellis recommended that a medical man be appointed to the Tramways Committee to examine men in their employ. He revealed that 'We have now no less than forty spare men to keep to take the places of those who fall sick.' The rules about drawing sick pay were rather severe. A man, other than an official, declaring himself unfit for work had first to forward a doctor's certificate. If the man's wages were 25 shillings a week, and his sick pay from the Sick Benefit Society 15 shillings, then the Corporation grant would be 50 per cent of the sick pay, bringing the total to 22s. 6*d*. But if his sick pay were 20 shillings a week, he would receive from the Corporation only 5s., as no man could receive more than his wages from both sources. However, members of the official staff, when unfit for duty, did get their full pay.

Traffic results for March 1905 showed that receipts were £8,314 5s. 8*d*.

compared with £8,093 6*s.* 3*d.* for the previous March, and the cars had carried 44,180 more passengers despite running 10,985 fewer miles. The deficit for the year ended 31st March, 1905, was about £1,400, but this included the deduction of loan charges and interest, and setting aside an amount for depreciation.

Cardiff received its City status on 28th October, 1905; and a very handsome coat of arms henceforth adorned the tramcars, with the words 'Awake, it is the day' and 'The Red Dragon will lead the way' in Welsh' (*Deffro maen Ddydd* and *Y Ddraig Goch Ddyry Cychwyn*).

Car No. 56 enters a section of interlaced track in The Hayes; it is working the Broadway (Newport Road) to Pier Head service, *c.* 1910. *Ernest T. Bush No. 3135*

Chapter Five

1906 to 1926

A short length of junction line at the southern end of St Mary Street, connecting Mill Lane to Penarth Road, was completed on 20th September, 1906. This work had been authorised nearly three years ago, to enable an occasional service of through cars to run from Grangetown to Queen Street via the Great Western railway station, but actually the two tracks were in practice used as terminal spurs, Penylan Road cars always using the west track and Salisbury Road cars the east one.

The Committee was warned not to go ahead with ill-considered extensions, merely on the strength of the success of principal routes. It was bad planning to divide traffic to one point over two routes; for example, Grangetown, which was quoted as having originally one profitable service, now had two, both of which made a loss, and a similar situation existed over the alternative routes to Splott.

From November 1906 the Tramways Committee was merged with the Electrical & Lighting Committee; this arrangement continued until 31st March, 1924, when they were again separated. So great was the Committee's confidence in Arthur Ellis, the Electrical Engineer & Tramways Manager, that in April 1907 he was granted absolute and sole control of managing the tramways system, without reference to the Corporation, for a year - his only restrictions being that he could not increase fares, or sack any official staff appointed by the Corporation.

Traffic receipts during this period were very satisfactory, and were achieved partly by withdrawing cars from unremunerative routes and placing them on routes where there was more traffic; and partly by readjusting fares. There were many anomalies; for example, fares on some routes were lower than on others; only an increase could allow the City Council to meet its heavy capital charges and set aside enough for renewals. The new fares started in July 1909 and a record year was the result, with a profit of £11,532 up to 31st March, 1910, compared with £5,954 the previous year. Against this, the track was wearing out very rapidly in places where there was intensive use, some sections having up to 676 cars daily, and these rails could not be expected to last more than three years; Mr W. Harpur, the city engineer, recommended spending £11,000 a year for track renewals instead of the usual £7,000, but the Committee resolved to increase the annual amount by only £1,000.

On 11th August, 1911, a Parcels Delivery Service started, after some years of delay and setbacks, for the idea had first been mooted at a Committee meeting on 9th December, 1904. The Post Office could not object, since the Corporation had power under its 1898 Act, and the service would be limited to within the borough. Ordinary service cars were used to carry the parcels, which could be up to 14 pounds in weight, and so long as up to 450 a week were carried, it was enough to pay expenses. The service was successful, and continued until 1942.

An important improvement late in 1912 was a plan submitted by the manager

Four-wheeled car No. 111, built by the Brush Electrical Engineering Co. in 1904, turns from Cowbridge Road into Cathedral Road about 1908. *Viner's Series No. 140*

Brush double-deck car No. 106 on service 2 (Pier Head to Newport Road) passes Milnes single-deck car No. 121 on the Whitchurch Road to St Mary Street (Service 1) in Queen Street. *Viner's Series No. 286*

for the numbering of routes, and displaying large figures on the cars to denote them. This was brought in in 1913.

The Chairman, now Sir John Courtis, announced that an important section of single track in Newport Road was to be doubled, but nothing had been done a year later (1914), since owners of the land to be purchased for road widening had imposed prohibitive terms, forcing the Council to apply for powers to purchase compulsorily.

The War had little effect on the tramways at first, but with the shortage of staff maintenance went down; only 80 cars could be used out of 130, and those with difficulty; pleasure riding more or less ceased, so receipts went down, and the track got steadily worse. Sir John Courtis opposed the policy of waiting for the war to end before doing repairs. 'Unless something was done they would soon have to start digging people and cars out of the roads.'

On 21st March, 1915, fortunately a Sunday, a 70-ton flywheel on one of the engines in the power station burst, and flying fragments damaged plant in the station, leaving a gaping hole in the wall and roof. An official statement issued by the Chairman and Manager was quoted in *Tramway & Railway World*:

> The accident took place at 6.25, and the cause of it is, so far, quite unascertainable. What has happened is that the engine carrying the load for the lighting service began to race, and the excessive speed of the flywheel consequent upon this resulted in the bursting of the wheel. Fragments of it, some weighing nearly a ton, were hurled through the roof and side of the building, causing considerable damage, and part of the switchboard was also damaged. It is very fortunate and providential that no one was hurt. It has been found impossible to resume the passenger service tonight, and on Monday the workmen's cars will not run in the early morning. It is, however, hoped that a restricted service will be commenced during the morning, and it is believed that the lighting arrangements will be fully resumed tonight.

First priority was to give temporary cover to the exposed machinery. Limited tramway services were started two days after the breakage. It was not explained why the machine ran at excessive speed; it was recommended that the wrecked engine be replaced by a turbine.

As in other towns, women had to be employed to keep the tramways going; two were trained as drivers, and there were many conductresses; by the end of the War there were 200 women on the tramways, but several were released as the men returned home. Because of the reduced service, the queue system was invented, and was successfully employed at key points, helping to speed up the service. Attempts were made to prevent people from pleasure riding or shopping during the busy periods, and threats were made that if they persisted in this anti-social practice the Corporation would demand proof from its passengers that they were engaged on work essential to the national interest. Fortunately it never came to that, as by May 1919 it was found possible to improve the service to some extent, with extra cars morning and evening, the service as a whole running from 5.10 am to 11 pm. Ellis had actually asked the Board of Trade for sanction to use trailers, an interesting speculation of what might have been; and this sanction was granted in August 1920, although never used.

A fine view of St Mary Street taken from the roof of the *Western Mail* building during an Edwardian high summer. Car No. 74 is seen approaching and bound for Pier Head, and the Wood Street junction is visible. On the skyline, St John's Church and the clock tower of City Hall. *Ernest T. Bush No. 2904*

St Mary Street about 1914, after route-indicating discs on the trams had been replaced by service numbers on metal plates; a car on service 5 (Victoria Park to Pier Head) is closely followed by one on service 6 (Cathedral Road to Clarence Road). *Viner's Series No. 285*

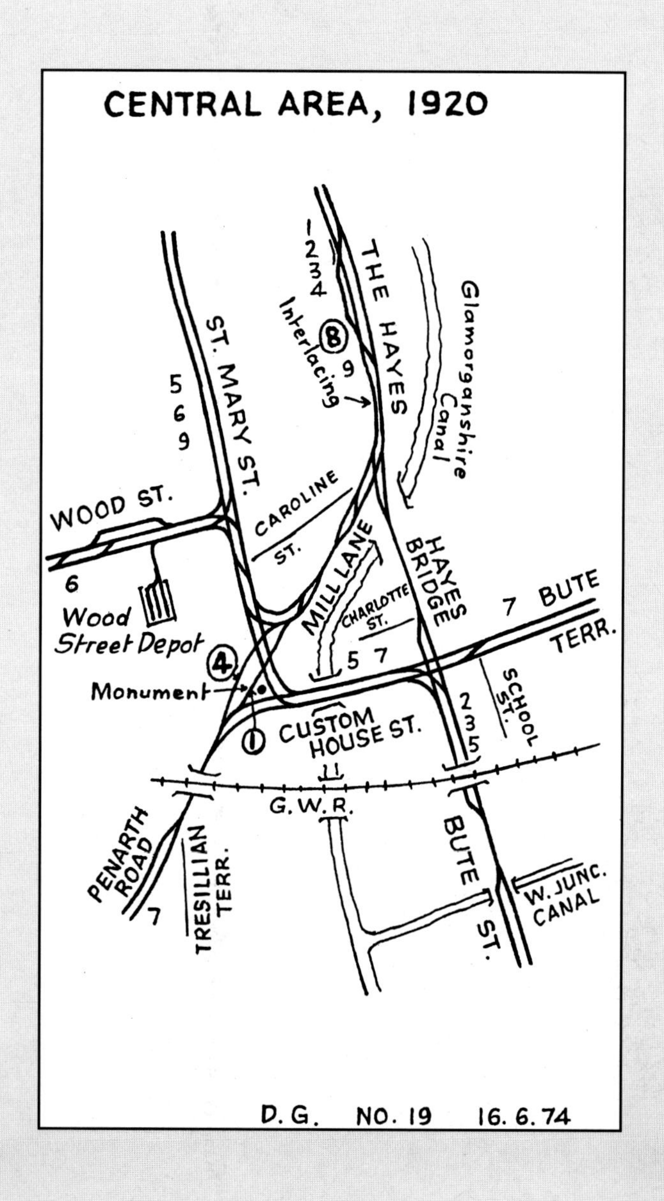
CENTRAL AREA, 1920
1
2
3
4
THE HAYES
Glamorganshire
Canal
Interlacing
8
9
5
6
9
ST. MARY ST.
WOOD ST.
CAROLINE
ST.
MILL LANE
HAYES
BRIDGE
6
Wood
Street Depot
CHARLOTTE
ST.
7
BUTE
TERR.
4
5 7
Monument
SCHOOL
ST.
1
CUSTOM
HOUSE ST.
2
3
5
G.W.R.
PENARTH
ROAD
7
TRESILLIAN
TERR.
BUTE
ST.
W. JUNC.
CANAL
D.G. NO. 19 16.6.74

Single-deck car No. 41 of 1902 on Service 7 (Carlisle Street, Splott, and Grangetown) in Adam Street, 1919. The bridge carrying the Taff Vale Railway over the street is behind the camera and the signals are reflected in the bulkhead window. Driver Middleton is at the controls, and the photograph was taken by E. Bowden, Inspector C.C.T. *Ian L. Wright Collection*

New top-covered car in Queen Street, outside the Eagle Star & British Dominions Insurance Company's building in 1924, immediately before the removal of the centre poles supporting the overhead and replacement by side poles and span-wires. The car, on service 4, is travelling from Market Road to Penylan Road. *Martin J. Ridley No 8590*

Yet another idea from the fertile mind of Arthur Ellis was his suggestion in March 1919 that the tramways of Cardiff and nearby Newport be linked within a few years. It would be necessary to extend tramways to outer suburbs in order to relieve the railways of this traffic and allow them to concentrate on long-distance traffic. However, a bus service was proposed instead, on which *Tramway & Railway World* commented: 'The entry to Newport is a reminder of Mr Arthur Ellis's foresight as to the need for light railways in the district. At last a practical means has been taken for testing and developing the traffic.'

Unfortunately, the 'temporary' bus service, when it started, remained a bus service, and still does. It was provided by Cardiff Corporation at first, but soon taken over by Newport Corporation who (through their new company) still work it today.

Until this time, Cardiff had been an all-tramway city, but was now applying for powers to run petrol-electric and trackless trolley buses as feeders to the trams, in conjunction with a Boundaries Extension Bill. Tramway extensions were not forgotten though: the Cardiff Parliamentary Committee directed the City Engineer and the Tramways Manager to include in the Bill powers to extend lines along Cowbridge Road to Ely; Whitchurch Road to North Road; Albany Road to Newport Road; Newport Road to Moira Place via Fitzalan Road; and through Duke Street after widening.

Early in 1920, Arthur Ellis retired to take up private practice, continuing to live in Cardiff. He was presented with a silver ink stand and tray by the Traffic Department administrative staff; he had devoted nearly 20 years to the tramways of Cardiff. His place was taken, from 8th March, 1920, by R.L. Horsfield, a Member of the Institute of Transport and native of Bradford, who had been employed from 1891 to 1902 on the Bradford & Shelf Steam Tramways Co., and since 1903 had been General Manager of Walsall Corporation Tramways.

By late 1920 100 cars were in service out of 130, and track renewal was going on as fast as possible. Traffic was increasing, with plenty of pleasure-riding; the renewals fund, accumulated between May 1902 and March 1920, amounted to £182,690; the debt repaid was £432,010, with £371,412 remaining to be paid.

Thoughts turned to purchasing new cars and, to keep costs down, Mr Horsfield advised that bodies and trucks be purchased separately and the cars be assembled by department staff at Roath Depot. As a stop-gap measure, several bogie cars were rebuilt with extended canopies, windscreens and curved stairways; this work was carried out at Roath.

Cardiff obtained its powers to run motor buses, anywhere inside the city and on three specified routes outside, by an Act of 16th August, 1920, 10 & 11 Geo. V, c.142, and placed six Tilling Stevens petrol-electric buses on the first route, St John Square and Monthermer Road, on 24th December, 1920. However, it would be a grave error to suppose that this action was the beginning of the end for the tramways; the buses were run only as feeders, or on low-traffic routes, and through the 1920s the tramways continued to develop.

This same 1920 Act also authorised construction of four new tramway extensions:

Two trams (Nos. 37 of 1925 and 108 of 1924) specially posed beneath Bute Street railway bridge to demonstrate the tiny amount of clearance between trolley-base and bridge.

Author's Collection

Brush covered-top car No. 111 on the Roath Park turning circle, 3rd March, 1926. In the background is the former Taff Vale Railway's Roath branch. *H.B. Priestley*

No. 1 6.80 chains, along Duke Street from Castle Street to Queen Street.
No. 2 1.15 chains, a curve from High Street into Duke Street.
No. 3 18.2 chains, along Fitzalan Road from Newport Road to Moira Place.
No. 4 51.4 chains, along Albany Road from Newport Road to Wellfield Road.

All four were to be wholly double track; Nos. 1 and 2 were not allowed to be built unless and until Duke Street was widened. Nos. 1 and 2 were in fact built, but Nos. 3 and 4 were not.

The Act also authorised the use of trailer cars and coupled cars, but the trackless trolley vehicles contemplated earlier were not included.

It will be recalled that Cardiff had not purchased the Whitchurch bus route of the Cardiff Tramways Company back in 1902, and this undertaking was still running the service, although now with motor buses instead of horse buses. However, the Corporation now wished to operate the Cardiff-Whitchurch service, and in August 1922 it purchased the company's land and buildings at Llandaff North for £6,000. The vehicles were not taken over. That a tramway company, after being forced to give up its operation of tramcars, should continue in being for another 20 years as a bus operator was rather unusual.

As from 31st March, 1923, ownership of the Tramways Power Station was transferred from the Tramways Committee to the Electricity Supply Department, and the Tramways thereafter purchased a bulk supply of 3,350 kw.

An illuminated car ran during Shopping Week from the 1st to 6th October, 1923; and during an Electrical Exhibition (21st to 31st January, 1925) two such cars were provided, one on the East side of the system and one on the West. For Shopping Week, 30th April to 9th May, 1925, a decorated car and bus, each with a band playing, were running, illuminated after dark. These undoubtedly beautiful displays continued a tradition begun with a decorated car run during the Coronation of 1911. They did not, however, carry passengers, being regarded as mobile tableaux.

During 1923-25 a total of 81 new totally-enclosed four-wheel double-deck cars and during 1926-27 a total of 31 new eight-wheel single-deck cars were purchased. These will all be described in detail in a later chapter.

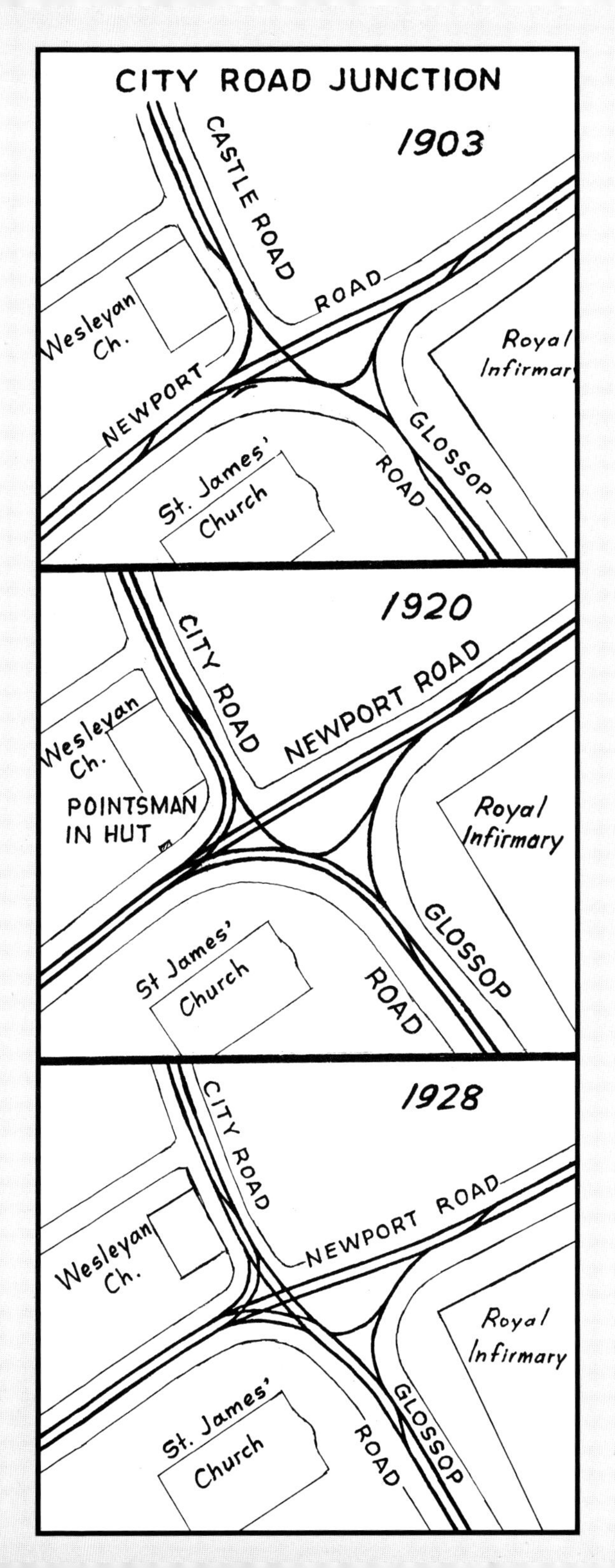
CITY ROAD JUNCTION
1903
CASTLE ROAD
ROAD
Wesleyan Ch.
NEWPORT
Royal Infirmary
GLOSSOP
ROAD
St. James' Church
1920
CITY ROAD
NEWPORT ROAD
Wesleyan Ch.
POINTSMAN IN HUT
Royal Infirmary
GLOSSOP
ROAD
St James' Church
1928
CITY ROAD
NEWPORT ROAD
Wesleyan Ch.
Royal Infirmary
GLOSSOP
ROAD
St. James' Church

Chapter Six

The Extensions

In the early 'twenties thoughts turned to extending one or two of the routes, partly to increase revenue, but mainly for the passengers' convenience. From this point of view, a proposal to extend the Cathedral Road line from its existing terminus at Berthwin Street to the entrance to Llandaff Fields was a sound one. What is hard to understand was how a scheme to build a tramway linking Ninian Road with Newport Road, running via Marlborough Road, ever received serious consideration, and indeed the residents of Marlborough Road got up a petition against the proposal, early in 1924.

Meanwhile, narrow Duke Street had been opened out; buildings on its north side were demolished, revealing a fine view of the Castle; at the same time, work went on with laying a double-line tramway in the new thoroughfare. The junction layout (Duke Street, Castle Street and High Street), supplied by Hadfields, cost £1,398; and the Titan Trackwork Co. provided the special work for Duke Street and Queen Street junction, at £510. Lt-Col. A.H.L. Mount inspected the completed line, which was opened on 4th June, 1924, by the Lord Mayor, Sydney Jenkins.

This short piece of line was a great improvement, as it saved trams from doing the long run from Queen Street to Castle Street via the Monument; there was thus a considerable saving in journey time.

In October 1926 six proposed extensions were considered:

No. 1 was a double line about 51 chains in length starting from Newport Road just east of Roath Court and terminating in Ninian Road, joining on to the existing tramway there.

No. 2 was a double or single line about 67 chains in length, being a continuation of the Whitchurch Road tramway from Talygarn Street and terminating in St Athan's Road, Gabalfa.

No. 3 was a double line of 10 chains along Moira Terrace, linking Moira Place with Meteor Street. Also included was a double line curve from Bute Terrace into Bute Street. This was to enable a direct service to run from the eastern termini to the Docks via Adam Street, avoiding the congestion in Queen Street and St John Square.

No. 4 was a double line 24 chains in length starting at the Cathedral Road terminus and to be taken to a point in Llandaff Fields 4 chains beyond the entrance.

The other two proposals were the first tentative steps in giving the city a modern tramway.

No. 5 was an extension from Victoria Park, along Cowbridge Road, then by means of a double-line sleeper track via Grand Avenue, Ely, to a point 24 chains west of Wilson Road.

No. 6 was a double line about 61 chains, starting at the junction of Penarth Road and Clive Street, along Penarth Road, then by means of a double-line sleeper track on the south-west side of Sloper Road to a point opposite Ninian Park Football Ground.

After debate, it was decided to apply to the Ministry of Transport for a Provisional Order for Extension Nos. 2, 3, 4 and 5; Nos. 1 and 6 were deleted and no more was heard of them. Nos. 1-4 had been authorised in previous Acts but the powers had by now expired.

The Cardiff Corporation Tramways Order Confirmation Act, 1927, duly became Law on 29th July, 1927, as 17 & 18 Geo. V, c 44, and authorised the construction of:

No. 1 67 chains, extending the Whitchurch Road tramway from Talygarn Street to and across North Road and then along St Athan's Road as far as Mynachdy Road. This was all to be double track except for two short sections of single at the northern end of Whitchurch Road; but it was not allowed to be built unless and until the section of Whitchurch Road from Canada Road to Newfoundland Road was widened to 32 ft 7 in. by setting back the kerb on one or both sides.

No. 2 12.12 chains, along Moira Terrace from Moira Place to Meteor Street, all to be double track.

No. 3 24.15 chains, extending the Cathedral Road tramway from Berthwin Street to the end of Cathedral Road, and continuing in a straight line along a proposed new street for six chains beyond the entrance to Llandaff Fields. This was all to be double track.

No. 4 2 miles 9.4 chains, extending the Cowbridge Road tramway from Victoria Park (and including the doubling of 3.45 chains of existing single track from Radnor Road to Clive Road), for about 1½ miles along Cowbridge Road, with a bridge over the Great Western Railway main line, then turning off to the north along Grand Avenue, and along an intended continuation of Grand Avenue (not yet built) as far as a point 21.5 chains west of Wilson Road. All this was to be double track except for 7.7 chains of single just beyond Mayfield Avenue and 2.65 chains of single just beyond Ely Road.

By September 1927 everything was ready for work to start on three of the extensions, but the fourth (Grand Avenue) was put off; perhaps doubts were entertained about its traffic potential. Mr Horsfield commented on the three that were to be built.

Tramway No. 1 - Whitchurch Road: 'One of our heavy traffic routes with a direct service to the Central Station.' Tramway No. 2 - Moira Terrace: 'A valuable improvement in our tramway system . . . The saving of time is an important factor, especially considering the traffic to the Docks.'

He was not quite so enthusiastic over Tramway No. 3 - Cathedral Road: 'Although it would be a more satisfactory terminus, I do not see that an extra fare could be charged . . . The greatest asset would be public convenience'.

It was decided not to extend the Whitchurch Road tramway as far as St Athan's Road but instead to make the Whitchurch Road terminus just short of the junction with North Road; the road at this point had to be widened to allow double track to be laid, and five forecourts were compulsorily purchased. Hadfields provided the following special work: crossovers, £664; and two sets of turnouts - for the single line section - at £310 each. On 15th June, 1928, the extension received an MOT inspection, and it opened the following day, service starting at 9.0 am.

Work on the Cathedral Road extension started about April 1928; it was quite

straightforward. However, a remarkable feature was the provision of scissors crossovers at the new terminus - a feature unusual on the system. They cost £796 10s. and were supplied by Hadfields. The Parks Committee, apparently nervous at the idea of trams actually running into the Fields to the public danger, requested the Tramways Committee to put up a fence either side of the tracks, but this was not done.

Opening date was 6th August, 1928. The *South Wales Echo* observed:

> Holiday-makers who visited Llandaff Fields had an agreeable surprise this morning. After taking the usual ticket to the terminus they found themselves borne beyond Berthwin Street and set down in the midst of the green expanses of one of Cardiff's favourite parks. The trams now stop within the Fields, and so the cars no longer stand in the middle of Cathedral Road - a death trap to motorists and pedestrians.

As foreshadowed by Mr Horsfield, no extra fare was charged, so the extension added nothing to revenue. Worse still, the entire length of Cathedral Road was used also by motor buses, running to the outer suburbs, so it would really have been more satisfactory to extend the tramway much further, so as to replace these buses.

Unfortunately for the future of Cardiff's tramways, R.L. Horsfield, now 54, resigned his managership, officially on 31st December, 1928, though he was allowed to leave three months before that date, and took up a similar post at Leeds. His place at Cardiff was taken by a man who had very different views on tramways - William Forbes, M.Inst.T., who had been manager of Aberdeen Corporation Tramways since 1918 and formerly chief assistant under that well-known busman R. Stuart Pilcher. Forbes's salary on appointment in Cardiff in December 1928 was £1,150 per annum.

With the change of manager came a change in policy; the Moira Terrace line was eventually completed in 1929, but never opened for regular traffic - the plan for fast trams to the Docks having been abandoned. However, it was retained for emergency working, and came in useful in 1949, as we shall see. Incidentally, all three extensions were paved in Mastic asphalt by Western Trinidad Lake Asphalt Co. The total cost of the lines was £29,328; of this, £558 came out of Revenue and the rest over a 20-year loan.

The Tramways Committee had now decided not to go ahead with the Ely extension, but were considering applying for an extension of time. Mr Forbes, the new manager, advised against it - and so Cardiff never got any reserved-track tramways. In May 1929 he presented the following report:

> It was inopportune at present for the proposed extension to be proceeded with in view of (1) High annual capital charges and estimated loss from operation of the proposed services; (2) Satisfactory financial position of Bus Services to the district combined with cheap fares and transfer ticket facilities; (3) That one of the present Bus Services would still require to be maintained - probably at a loss; (4) That in the event of further growth of the Estate as far as St Fagans Road, Buses would have to be operated for the transport of passengers to and from the tramway cars; and (5) That the excessive standing charges at present burdening the Undertaking would still further be increased, without any compensating financial advantage.

So the era of expansion, brief as it was, was over. From now on it was going to be retrenchment, although there was as yet no thought of actually abandoning the entire system. Cardiff Corporation Tramways were at their maximum extent for less than a year.

Cardiff Corporation Tramways and Motor Omnibuses.

Mr. R. M. Pittard

loyally served the Citizens during the period of the

National Emergency

(May 3rd – 14th 1926) as a

Volunteer Conductor

At a Civic Reception held on Friday, the 16th July, 1926, the Volunteers were Publicly Thanked for their Services and the above-named Volunteer was presented with this Souvenir in recognition of his faithful adherence to the ideals of True Citizenship.

[illegible] Lord Mayor.

Chapter Seven

The General Strike and its Aftermath

Obeying instructions from their Union headquarters, all tramwaymen in Cardiff (and elsewhere) ceased work on and from Tuesday, 4th May, 1926, in support of the coalminers. On the first day most Cardiff citizens had to walk; private bus owners provided a full service, but there were no municipal trams or buses at all. Mr Horsfield received many applications from volunteers who were willing to risk their persons for the delights of a chance to indulge in tram-driving.

Work continued in the power station, but it was thought that if power were used to run trams, the men would *go out*. On the second day, buses were being run by volunteer drivers; police prevented pickets from unseating one driver. On the morning of the 6th, the power station men walked out, but work was carried on by officials. Shortly after 3 pm the first tramcar appeared, driven by no less a person than Arthur Ellis. More cars appeared, and a service was provided until 8 pm. The manager had a list of 90 drivers and prospective conductors, many of whom were old employees. The City Council notified the tramwaymen on strike that they must either return to work or return their uniforms by Friday; the Council did not regard the strike as an ordinary one, but as a concerted movement against society. Over a dozen men resumed work on Friday 7th May; none of the others returned his uniform.

An attempt was made to assault a tram driver and conductor, but a baton charge by police soon dispersed the crowd. There was, in fact, surprisingly little violence; some missiles were thrown at buses and cars, and one volunteer driver was hit on the leg with an iron bar.

But now, the strikers had become disillusioned; they saw that they were getting nowhere, and were angry with those who had conned them into risking losing their jobs; and on Monday, 10th May, most of them resumed their duties. 114 men reported by 1 pm, and 29 trams and 34 buses were in service; by 6 pm 300 men were working and 50 trams and all buses were out. The *Western Mail*, which had been one of the very few newspapers to continue publication during this period, and whose appearance had astonished the country, jubilantly announced that the tram-men's strike had collapsed.

On the 11th 51 cars and 36 buses were in service, on all routes. There were still plenty of volunteers, as some strikers had not returned. Mr Horsfield stated: 'Approximately 160 old employees have returned for duty. Some are driving trams or buses; a large number of others are engaged in teaching recruits to drive.'

The General Strike officially ended on 12th May 1926. Any volunteer who wished to stay on in permanent employment could do so, if suitable, and some forty men were thus engaged. This action was severely criticised by the Tramways Committee, as some of these men were almost at retiring age. The Committee criticised the General Manager for being absent in London shortly before the strike started, and for not being in closer touch with his officials. The

Two single-deck cars on Service 7 pass at Penarth Road/Custom House Street on 20th April, 1927. No. 101 travelling to Roath Dock, Splott is new, but the other car, bound for Clive Street Grange, is a reconditioned 1902 bogie tram. *H. B. Priestley*

During April 1927 City Road was isolated from the rest of the system because of the reconstruction of City Road junction. Nineteen cars provided a shuttle service until 9th May. This line-up of cars is headed by No. 142, a bogie car recently renumbered, in City Road on 19th April, 1927. *H.B. Priestley*

Lord Mayor had taken the initiative, and the Committee was very grateful. Sydney Jenkins - who had been Chairman since 1921 - for being absent in London 'at a critical time' also earned the disapproval of his Committee, who actually asked him to resign his Chairmanship, which he did. W.R. Williams was Chairman from June 1926; nine months later Sydney Jenkins was dead.

All volunteers not wishing to take permanent employment were sent a personal letter of thanks by the Lord Mayor. There is little doubt that the volunteers regarded the episode as 'a bit of a lark', but the Corporation was more than grateful to them, as in those days service to the public was regarded as the primary consideration.

In 1927 the Transport Offices were moved from The Hayes to Dragon Buildings, Paradise Place - quite a name. Negotiations with the GWR were begun, on a proposal to raise the bridge in Adam Street to allow double-deck cars to run. Work on this was carried out during 1929.

The GWR was approached about Salisbury Road bridge, and asked whether it would be prepared to raise it. Mr Horsfield prepared a report in June 1928 showing that, if double-deck cars could be used, the service could be reduced from every 6 minutes to 8; because these cars were faster, the journey time could be reduced by 2 minutes for each journey, or 4 minutes the round trip, using three fewer cars on the same number of journeys. As mentioned in the previous chapter, Mr Horsfield left Cardiff in September 1928, and from December the new General Manager was Mr William Forbes - who was distinctly not in favour of tramway route extensions.

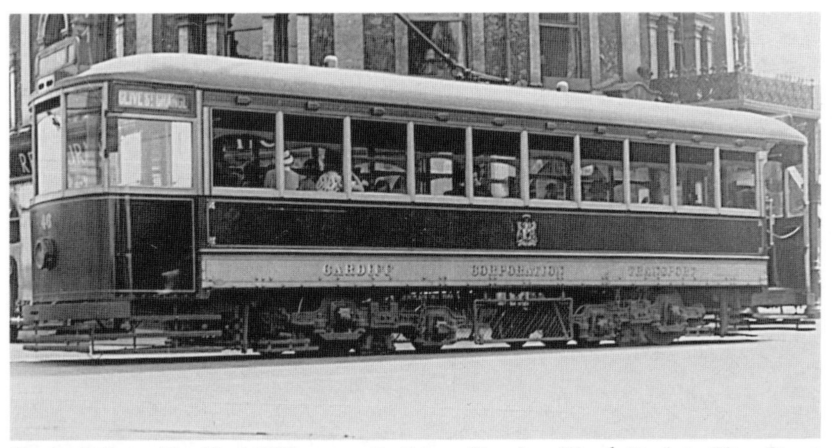

Single-deck car No. 46 of 1927 on service 7 travelling from Roath Dock to Clive Street Grange, leaving Custom House Street and about to enter Penarth Road. *Hugh Nicol*

Taken in the late 1920s, this picture shows new single-deck car No. 52 working service 1A (Cathedral Road and Whitchurch Road), which was introduced in 1924.

Pier Head, Bute Street, and car No. 85 on service 3 to Roath Park reverses on one of the crossovers while another car waits to leave for Victoria Park on Service 5, 4th September, 1935.

H.B. Priestley

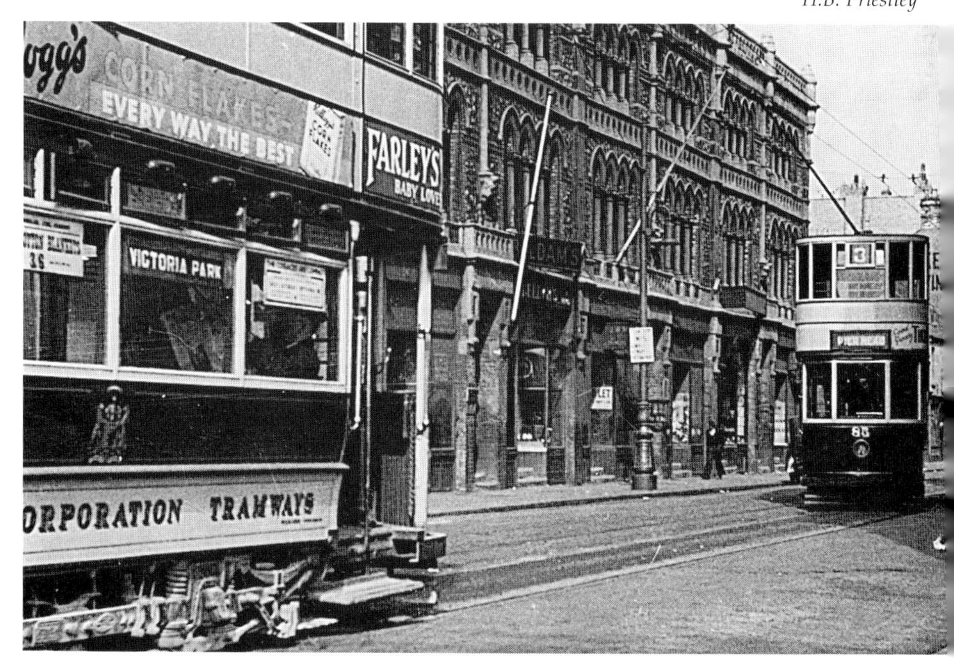

Chapter Eight

William Forbes' Managership

After recommending that the Ely tramway extension not be proceeded with, Forbes turned his attention to Salisbury Road. The GWR was not prepared to raise the bridge; the alternative, lowering the roadway, would be expensive and the risk of flooding would be present. In July 1929 he pointed out that ten lightweight double-deck buses of a low-height design could replace the twelve single-deck trams on this route; and in September the Committee decided that this should be done. The last day of the Salisbury Road tramway was 4th January, 1930; the replacing bus service was numbered 39 and ran from St Mary Street to St Athan's Road, Gabalfa, with wasteful bus/tram duplication along the whole of Whitchurch Road, including the recently-laid tramway extension.

During the six months ended 30th September, 1930, there was an apparent loss on tramway working of £3,849 and a profit on the buses of £3,851. Since Forbes had taken over, economies had been made in the running of the department; for example, instead of buying new tower wagons, the department had knocked up two using old petrol-electric bus chassis with the towers and bodywork of the former battery vehicles; then, when the mobile welder wore out, a new one was converted from a withdrawn double-deck bus body for £10.

Although one tram route had been closed, there were not as yet any plans to scrap the whole system. The Chairman, Henry Johns, said that there would be a gradual move towards motor buses; and each route would be considered separately when the need for track reconstruction arose. Some thought it would be a good idea to abandon the Monument-Clive Street section, in connection with the GWR's rebuilding of General station and the railway bridge over Penarth Road during 1931, but Forbes pointed out that the track had a further life expectancy of over five years, and that the tramcars on the route were modern. As he had managed the undertaking so carefully and economically he was awarded a salary increase of £250 per annum.

It is interesting to note that, in Cardiff, no byelaws existed requiring drivers of vehicles to stop while passengers were boarding or alighting from trams (or buses!) and that proposals in local Bills to empower local authorities to make such byelaws were consistently disallowed by Parliament at this time. The point is made to emphasise the fact that motor traffic was increasing, and stepping into the road at busy points of the city was becoming rather dangerous. Hope was expressed that motorists would drive with due care for tramway passengers.

The Cardiff Corporation Act of 1934 was passed on 31st July, 1934, as 24 & 25 Geo. V, c.95. It was a general Act for the whole city, not just the tramways, but among the 83 clauses was one (No. 20) which was of considerable importance to the future of the tramways.

It stated that the Corporation might provide and maintain trolley vehicles but should not manufacture them; and it might use them on the whole or any part of the existing Corporation Tramways, and on any other street or road

Wood Street and 'Temperance Town', looking west, *c*. 1937. On the left is the siding leading to the former horse-tram depot. The boarded-up shops are about to be demolished and demolition has already occurred further along the street. *Author's Collection*

The Hayes, showing fruit market, statue of John Batchelor 'the friend of freedom', the slip-points and car No. 9 on service 2, Newport Road to Pier Head, on 6th April, 1937. *H.B. Priestley*

City Road junction, looking north-east. City Road to left, Newport Road ahead, and Glossop Road to right. Car No. 94 is seen on Service 2A travelling from Victoria Park to Newport Road terminus, 6th April, 1937. *H.B. Priestley*

Queen Street bridges: in the foreground is the former Taff Vale Railway bridge and behind is the former Rhymney Railway one. Four separate excursions for 12th September, 1937, plus one on the 15th, are advertised. Car No. 100 on service 4 from St Mary Street to Roath Park passes under the low bridges on 14th September, 1937. *H.B. Priestley*

Newport Road/Broadway on 7th September, 1937, with car No. 80 on Service 2A to Victoria Park about to pass a car on Service 2B (St Mary Street to Newport Road). Four seated gentlemen are enjoying the sun but do not seem interested in the trams. *H.B. Priestley*

Whitchurch Road terminus, looking north-west on 14th September, 1937; car No. 37 on service 1 to Cathedral Road. On the right, St Mark's vicarage, demolished in the early 1960s. *H.B. Priestley*

necessary or convenient for providing a turning point or for access to a depot. The Corporation was empowered to abandon or discontinue either temporarily or permanently any existing tramway on its being replaced by trolley vehicles.

Disappointingly, no illuminated car ran during the Silver Jubilee of 1935, as none could apparently be spared; the only decoration allowed was pennants tied to trolley booms.

During 1936, track was removed in Mundy Place, Wyeverne Road, Salisbury Road and St Andrew's Place. Charge to the now-renamed Transport Committee for reinstating Woodville Road was approximately £250. It was reported that the track between Splott Bridge and Portmanmoor Road terminus was in very bad condition, and the General Manager was asked to report on the future of the Splott-Grangetown route. There were three choices - track reconstruction; substitution of trackless trolley buses; or substitution of oil-engined buses. The route had seen a car mileage reduction of nearly 240,000 during 1934-5, and had made a profit of £3,330.

> In view of the above, and also to the estimated additional profit of £5,777 from operation of heavy-oil buses, against a loss on either trams, after reconstruction, or trackless trolley buses, I recommend that the tram track from Adamsdown Square to Portmanmoor terminus should be scrapped, and heavy-oil buses substituted for trams, and that the tramway services be re-organised . . .
>
> The only portion of the Roath Dock-Clive Street tramway track which would require to be retained would be between Adamsdown Square, Moira Terrace, Adam Street, Custom House Street, to St Mary Street. This part of the track was in good order and would prove useful in the event of breakdowns in Queen Street and diversions of service which frequently take place. As there would not be any further use for the single-deck trams, they could all be dispensed with to the best advantage, and the price realised credited to Capital Account.

Forbes's report was accepted without a murmur of dissent, even though the single-deck cars were but 10 years old, whilst 20 Cathays buses ordered in 1929 were already worn out and 20 more were needed. Eleven buses were ordered for the Splott-Grangetown route, for delivery in October 1936, and nobody seemed to think it was a poor investment. Buses took over on Sunday, 11th October, 1936, on service 7, Splott to Grangetown via Adam Street, and 12, Splott to Avondale Road via Queen Street. Bus service 12a, Willows Avenue (Splott) to St Mary Street, started next day. Passengers continued to enjoy facilities previously provided, such as workmen's and season tickets. The Splott track was eventually lifted and a concrete road surface put down.

For the Coronation of 1937, the General Manager recommended using an illuminated bus, but no illuminated tram, because of 'congestion'. It was difficult to operate even normal services through Queen Street on some days. All trams were decorated with flags and 20 were 'specially decorated' with bunting and flags. All car sheds, depots and offices were decorated. On the 13th May, 1937, the Transport Department displayed Tableaux depicting 'Transport through the Ages'; the procession included an Ark (BC 2448) on a petrol chassis, a Coach and Four (1814), a petrol-electric bus (1914), and the latest oil-engined bus; but it does seem unfair that no tram was included.

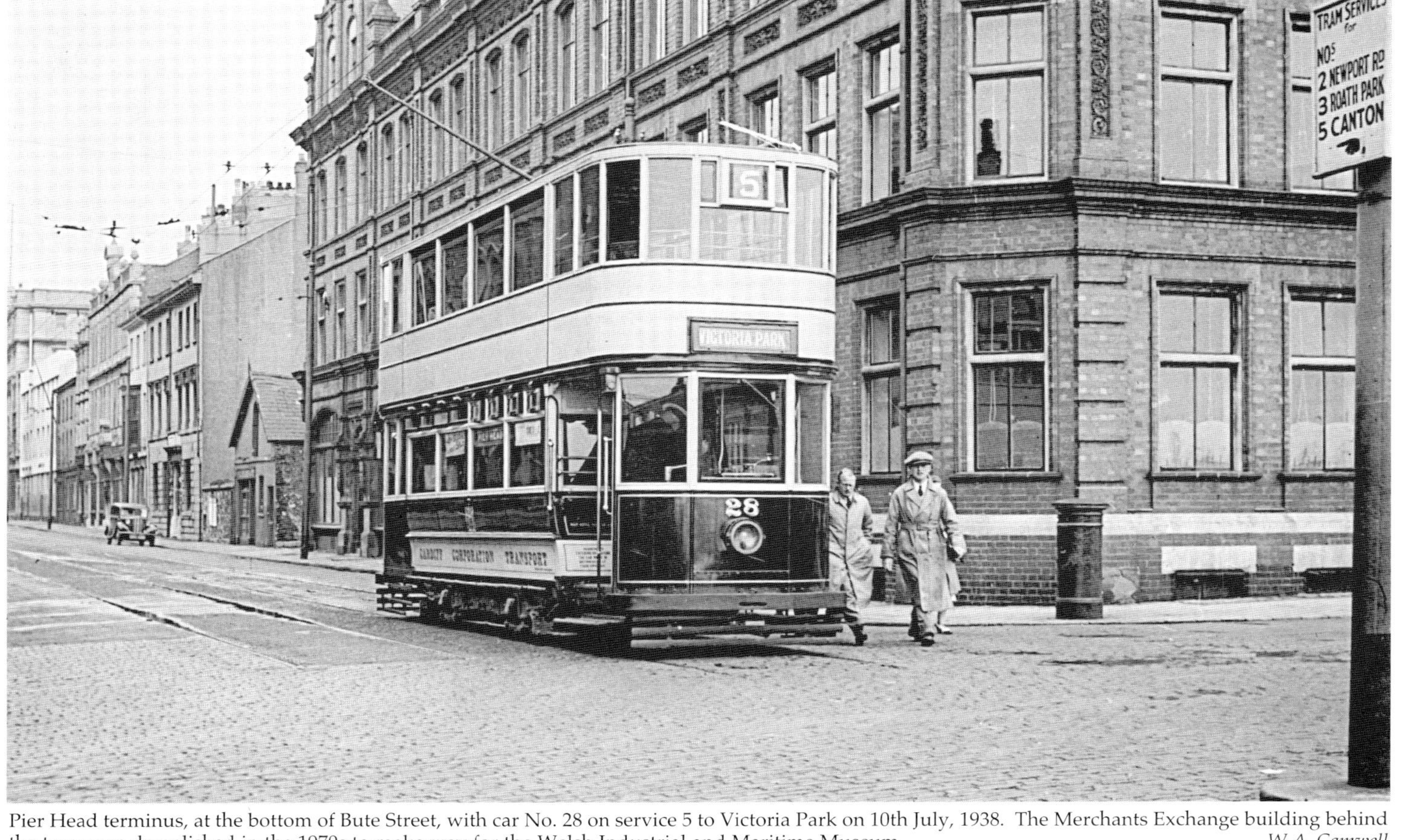

Pier Head terminus, at the bottom of Bute Street, with car No. 28 on service 5 to Victoria Park on 10th July, 1938. The Merchants Exchange building behind the tram was demolished in the 1970s to make way for the Welsh Industrial and Maritime Museum. *W.A. Camwell*

Car No. 69 in Newport Road, just outside Roath Depot; note the recording clock to the right.
C.F. Klapper

The tree-lined Cathedral Road is one of Cardiff's finest streets. Here is car No. 31 on service 6 to Clarence Road being overtaken by a bus on service 24 (Llandaff Circular), 7th April, 1938.
H.B. Priestley

Roath Park terminus, looking south-east. Cars 26 and 89 on service 4 in 1938. *W.A. Camwell*

One of five Dick, Kerr 4-wheeled trams rebuilt with extended canopies, vestibules and new Peckham Pendulum truck: No. 13 stands in Clare Road outside the depot, 10th July, 1938. The 'passengers' are friends of the photographer. *W.A. Camwell*

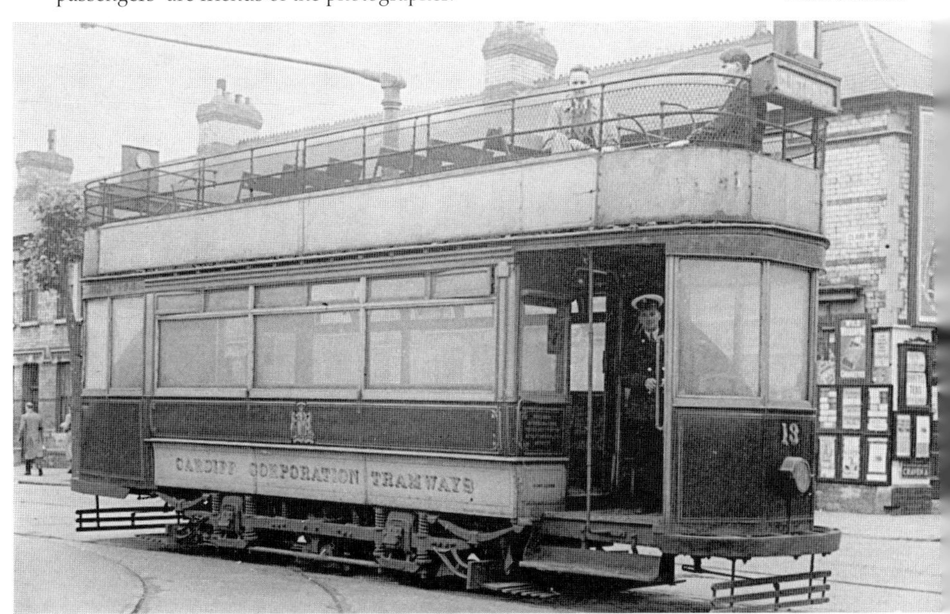

Wood Street, along which the No. 6 service passed, ran through a sordid area known as Temperance Town, so called because the building of public houses had been forbidden when the land was reclaimed from the Taff River and the dwellings built in 1858; and it was now proposed to redevelop the area, in furtherance of which the Transport Committee was asked if it would consider discontinuing tramway operation in Wood Street. In May 1937 the Transport Committee stated that it was in favour of doing so. William Forbes's report had indicated that there was very little debt on the tracks from Wood Street to Clarence Road, and so he prepared alternative schemes for (A) motor buses, replacing the No. 6 tram route (Llandaff Fields, Wood Street and Clarence Road), plus an extension of the Willows Avenue-St Mary Street service to Clarence Road; and (B) trolley buses, replacing the No. 6 tram route, with an intermediate service running from the Monument to Clarence Road. With oil-engined buses, he estimated an annual net profit of £4,044; and with trolley buses, a loss of £799. He would retain the Cathedral Road track for the time being.

The Transport Committee was still very happy to heed the advice of the General Manager, and would have gone ahead with substitution of buses; but the Finance Committee desired trolley buses, and said so, much to Henry Johns's annoyance. In March 1939, when the chairman of the Finance Committee said the decision should be taken out of the hands of the Transport Committee, Johns told him:

> I should be glad if you would. You are interfering and dictating a policy to a particular committee. I am getting so sick and tired of it that you can do what you like. It is time the city treasurer ran the transport system. He seems to know more about transport than the manager.

By this time it was more or less decided that the whole system should be abandoned; but the final decision on this rested with the City Council. On 8th May, 1939, the Council issued its decree, having decided by 37 votes to 14:

> That this Council, having considered the reports of the Transport Manager and the City Treasurer and Controller on the question of substitution of trams by oil or trolley buses, decides in favour of trolley buses and instructs the Transport Committee to take immediate steps to put this into effect.

Forbes prepared plans for tramway abandonment, with the worst tracks going first, and the best last. Clarence Road to Llandaff Fields would be a through trolley bus service, and tram service 1 - Llandaff Fields and Whitchurch Road - would continue, he hoped, for a short time only.

The start of World War II meant that 34 single-deck and 6 double-deck trams, in store at Roath Depot, would not be disposed of for the time being. The system was now in such a good way financially that it was found possible to reduce tram fares to only two levels - 1*d*. and 1½*d*. For the year ended 31st March, 1939, the net profit had been £11,979. The new fares started on 1st October; at once the number of passengers increased, but revenue went down. However, passenger figures went on increasing until the revenue became even

South-east end of Cathedral Road, with car No. 107 on service 1 to Whitchurch Road causing a minor delay to motor traffic as passengers alight on 9th April, 1938. *H.B. Priestley*

Cathedral Road terminus, showing the short extension into the entrance of Llandaff Fields - Cardiff's only 'reserved track'. Car No. 25 waits to leave for Clarence Road via Wood Street on service 6 in July 1938. *W.A. Camwell*

One of the two single-line sections in Cowbridge Road: this is near King's Road, looking west. Car 70 on Service 2A for Newport Road approaches. Will Hay's latest film, *Old Bones of the River*, is being shown at the Empire, Queen Street: 19th April, 1939. *H.B. Priestley*

Car No. 107 turns from Clare Road into Tudor Street, probably on a depot working. Service 1 (displayed) ran from Whitchurch Road to Cathedral Road, so this car was 'off route' when caught on 19th April, 1939. *H.B. Priestley*

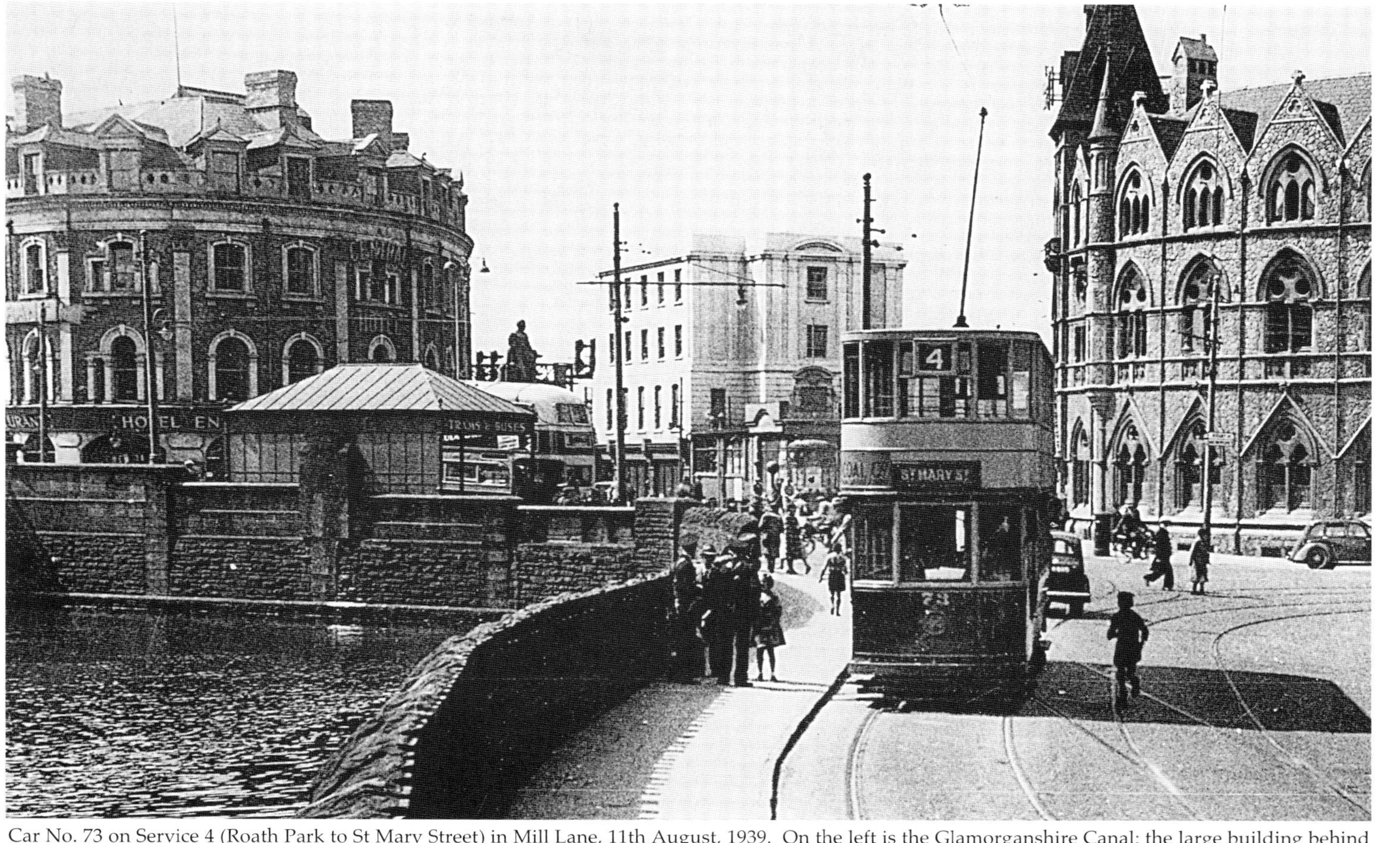

Car No. 73 on Service 4 (Roath Park to St Mary Street) in Mill Lane, 11th August, 1939. On the left is the Glamorganshire Canal; the large building behind is the Central Hotel and that to the right is the Great Western Hotel.

Victoria Park terminus on 19th April, 1939, showing car No. 68 at the end of the single-track stub. As it reverses, its trolley will be turned by the automatic trolley reverser in the wiring. Lansdowne Road, coming in on the left, joins Cowbridge Road; in the distance is Ely Paper Mill.
H.B. Priestley

On the Roath Park line, 9th April, 1939. Car No. 33 turns from Wellfield Road into Ninian Road while No. 114 waits. The track to Penylan Road is seen leading off to the right. *H.B. Priestley*

higher than before, with the old system; meanwhile, bus services had been reduced by half.

William Forbes died on 30th May, 1940, aged 57; although clearly a busman, he had undoubtedly been successful as General Manager of a combined tramway and bus undertaking. His careful and efficient management had consistently placed the Department in an excellent financial position.

In 1939 both the City Council and at least some members of the Transport Committee were becoming very enthusiastic about trolley buses, and so they applied for and obtained the Cardiff Corporation (Trolley Vehicles) Order Confirmation Act of 1940. This received the Royal Assent on 17th July, 1940, as 3 & 4 Geo. VI , c.36, and authorised an enormous network of no fewer than 56 miles 45 chains of new trolley bus route extensions entirely within the city boundary. Powers already existed from the 1934 Act to run trolley buses on 13 miles of tramway routes, so this gave a total of 69½ miles of authorised routes. It would have meant Cardiff becoming the second-largest operator of trolley buses in Britain, after London. After the War enthusiasm seemed to have evaporated and trolley buses in the main were confined to former tram routes, all of which served streets with high-density housing; beyond the tram termini were miles of newer suburbs with low-density housing, the serving of which by trolley buses would almost certainly have been uneconomic. These outer suburbs continued, therefore, to be served by motor buses and the trolley bus system only ever attained a maximum of 17¼ route miles.

The only trolley bus extensions beyond former tram termini were to Ely and to Pengam. The Ely extension, built in 1955, revived memories of the Cowbridge Road to Grand Avenue tramway authorised in 1927 but never built; the extension from Newport Road (Roath Depot) to Pengam was very short, and done more for operating convenience than any other reason.

Chapter Nine

The P.A.Y.E. Era

Shortly after the death of William Forbes, it was decided to separate the management of the traffic and engineering sides of the undertaking; thus William John Evans, from Rotherham, was appointed chief engineer with a salary of £800 a year, and John Weir Dunning, Member of the Institute of Transport, became traffic manager, also at a salary of £800. Mr Dunning had been chief traffic assistant to the tramways in 1927 and traffic superintendent since 1928; and since Forbes's death, acting General Manager. There was now no General Manager as such.

Passenger traffic was enormous at this period; so much so that it was felt that fares could be further reduced, to just one penny - in short, a flat fare. It was considered that there was a moral obligation to provide cheap transport for workers displaced to the outer areas by compulsory demolition of dwellings in the inner area. The choice of one penny as the fare to be used was not an arbitrary one, but represented the average fare paid previously.

The really revolutionary aspect of the scheme, however, was the use of coinboxes to collect fares, a conductor being retained solely to supervise the platform of the car, bus or trolleybus. Cardiff's first trolleybus service, No. 6 (Wood Street and Clarence Road) started operation on 1st March, 1942 (extended to Llandaff Fields on 8th November, 1942); and the Pay as you Enter system was introduced on this route on the same date. It was soon extended to all tram routes and selected bus routes.

The P.A.Y.E. device was designed and patented by W.J. Evans, in conjunction with East Lancashire Coachbuilders, of Blackburn. The assembly was mounted on the platform, just in front of the stair-well, and comprised two coinboxes, one on the staircase stringer, for upper-deck passengers, and one for lower-deck passengers, mounted on the bulkhead, both connected to a locked cash-box.

Each coin box had a glass front and sides, to enable the conductor to check the tendered fares, which were inserted through a slot in the metal top. The back of the box was fitted with a housing for an electric lamp, whose light was directed towards the coin slot and base of the box by means of openings in the back wall of the box.

The base of the coin box was actually a hinged flap, normally kept horizontal by means of a balance weight attached to a lever arm; a 'baffle plate' located within the box above the flap hinge directed coins to the centre of the flap. When a set weight of coins was on the flap, the deadweight was counter-balanced and the flap moved downward, releasing the coins.

The lower end of each box was fitted with a funnel-shaped extension, to which was clamped flexible metal tubing leading to the cash box, which was a drawer secured within a locker bolted to the floor. Every night, two labourers opened the lockers with a standard key, and removed the cash boxes, which were self-locking, incidentally, and took them to the depot office where they were unlocked by a trusted official. The coins were then machine-counted and

Car No. 60 in Queen Street on service 2 (Newport Road to Pier Head) on 1st August, 1940. The tram has a blackout mask over the headlamp and the fender is painted white, but the vehicle is still in immaculate condition. *H.B. Priestley*

Car No. 86 at Roath Park about 1940; blackout mask on headlamp and white-painted fender. The car has arrived from St Mary Street on service 4 and is about to return there. *Author's Collection*

bagged, and in the morning paid into the Department's bank. It was soon discovered that the enormous load of copper being paid caused problems, so arrangement was made that all the city banks should take the money in turn, in order to get it back into circulation quickly.

Each cash box was numbered; the only paper-work involved was a return showing the amount of cash in each box and which vehicle carried the box. There was also a daily way-bill for each vehicle, showing the services worked and the conductor's identity. Ticket inspectors were unnecessary as there were no tickets; only traffic inspectors were needed, traffic figures being derived from special observations and sample counts.

The conductor did not take any money or give any change; his only duty was to supervise the platform, which he did from a standing position just inside the lower saloon, on the off-side of the gangway. If passengers did not have the right money they just had to put in silver, and an overpayment slip would be issued and a refund made after the money had been counted.

Some advantages of the P.A.Y.E. system have been indicated; but there were many more. It meant that maximum-capacity vehicles could be used when they were not tied to the conductor's ability to collect a certain number of fares in a certain time; it meant fewer missed fares, and elimination of fare disputes; it improved passenger discipline, because of the need to form two lines for pre-payment, the boarding time being reduced to one second per passenger, resulting in a faster service speed; and it resulted in increased revenue, because of the vast number of passengers the cheap fare attracted.

Thus the system could be successful on short, heavily-trafficked routes and tram services were re-arranged to suit the P.A.Y.E. From 3rd May, 1942, these were arranged to terminate in the city centre, and P.A.Y.E. was introduced on them during 1943: Route 16 (Pier Head-The Hayes) on 7th March; 5A (St Mary Street-Victoria Park) and 8 (Victoria Park-Windsor Place) on 2nd May; and 1A/B (Whitchurch Road), 2A/B (Newport Road) and 4A/B (Roath Park) on 1st August, 1943.

On the night of Tuesday, 3rd September, 1940, Cardiff suffered its first serious air raid of World War II. Several houses were damaged in the Cathays district and in Albany Road shops were damaged, the debris obstructing the tram tracks and preventing any trams from running next morning and for several days after. Eleven people were killed and 35 injured during the bombing. Although the track itself was not damaged in Albany Road, services to Roath Park were not resumed until Friday, 13th September, trams being diverted until then to the former Talygarn Street terminus on the Whitchurch Road route and displaying service numbers 3 and 4.

During this period new automatic overhead trolley reversers were installed at Woodville Road junction, at Whitchurch Road Barracks and in Albany Road near City Road junction.

The tramways did not suffer a great deal from bombing, although the Central Offices at Paradise Place were destroyed on 2nd January, 1941, and a bomb just outside Roath Depot killed the store-keeper, Ivor Salisbury. Some trams received a dreary 'wartime grey' livery, and the windows at first were covered with fine matting, glued on, with a peephole 12 in. by 4 in. The matting was

A wartime scene in Wood Street, looking towards St Mary Street. Two cars fitted with blackout masks on the headlights, netting over the windows and with white-painted fenders, wait to work service 6a to Clarence Road on 21st August, 1941. *W.A. Camwell*

Morning rush hour at Victoria Park, 25th March, 1946. The bogie open-top cars were still in use at certain times; here No. 84 is about to work through to Roath depot. *Ian L. Wright*

removed about 1942.

A sudden and heavy snowfall on 25th January, 1945, severely disrupted tram and bus services but after gangs of men - including German prisoners of war - had cleared the snow the trams got through.

The end of the War found the tramways in a deplorable state. Because none of the track had been renewed the trams rode very badly and noisily, earning for themselves the disapproval of passengers and other citizens alike. Replacement was imperative, but the trams had to keep going for a few more years because post-war shortages held up construction of new trolley buses.

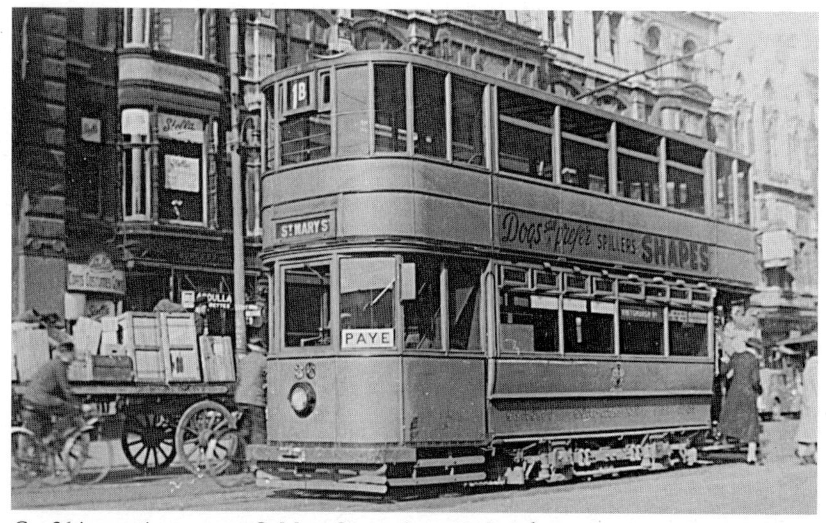

Car 36 in wartime grey at St Mary Street about 1946. It has arrived on service 1B from Whitchurch Road via Duke Street and will return to Whitchurch Road via The Hayes.
Author's Collection

Rebuilt bogie car No. 84, together with its driver, near the entrance of Roath depot, 20th February, 1945. *Ian L. Wright*

Chapter Ten

The Final Years

The experiment of joint management came to an end in 1946, and J.W. Dunning became sole General Manager, whilst W.J. Evans left Cardiff to become General Manager of Reading Corporation Transport. Also in 1946 the tracks in Neville Street and Lower Cathedral Road were removed, and Clare Road Depot was closed to trams on 25th August.

On 27th April, 1946, the last trams ran on route 16 to Pier Head, motor buses taking over the following day; from 17th August, 1947, seven 1930-built ex-Pontypridd Urban District Council six-wheel single-deck trolley buses operated this service until 1949, when five new six-wheel single-deck vehicles arrived.

Tram service 8 (Windsor Place to Victoria Park) ceased on 24th January, 1948, being replaced by a temporary motor bus the following day. Trams still ran to Canton on route 5A until 5th June, 1948, but by now enough trolley buses had arrived to enable them to take over this service from Sunday 6th June of that year. Trolley buses ran on Victoria Park-Windsor Place service from 4th July, 1948, now renumbered 5.

This left just the three Eastern routes in the city, being worked by 45 double-deck trams. The Newport Road line was next on the list, despite the fact that the track and wiring would have to be kept until the end because of the position of Roath Depot, Clare Road having been closed to trams. So, apart from depot journeys, Newport Road ceased to be worked by trams on 16th October, 1948, motor buses taking over on routes 2A and 2B the following day, and trolley buses from 15th October, 1950. Roath Depot was being converted for use by trolley buses during 1948.

The Department had hoped to cease tramway operation by June 1949, but non-delivery of trolley bus bodies gave the final two routes several months' reprieve. Unfortunately, car overhauls ceased and the trams got into an amazing state of decrepitude considering their 25 years' life; the car sides would move independently of the seats as the tram moved along over the appalling track. The public and the Press reviled the trams as never before.

On 27th March, 1949, there was a joint Southern Counties Touring Society and Light Railway Transport League tour of the remaining routes - the only occasion when a special tram had been chartered for such a purpose in Cardiff. Recently-painted car No. 88 was used.

It was necessary to lower the roadway under the Queen Street bridges for a 16 ft 6 in. headroom for trolley buses, and, rather than re-lay tram track, the department decided to re-route the trams via City Road junction, Moira Terrace and Adam Street to the bottom of St Mary Street, where an automatic trolley reverser was installed. The Adam Street track, which, as will be recalled, had been retained by Forbes for emergency use back in 1936, was still in excellent condition as it had seldom been used. Thus, the tramway tracks in Queen Street, Duke Street, High Street, The Hayes, and the greater part of St Mary Street were abandoned on 11th July, 1949, and services 1 and 4 diverted along

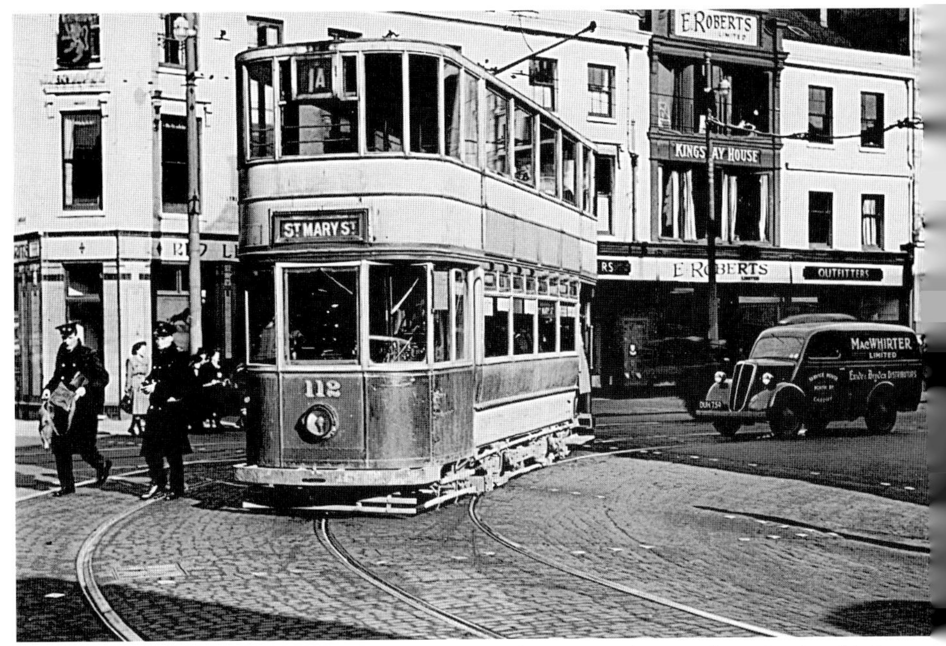

Car No. 112 turns from Queen Street into St John Street while working Service 1A from Whitchurch Road to St Mary Street, 10th February, 1949. *Ian L. Wright*

Car No. 67 at Roath Park on service 4A from St Mary Street in the post-war period. Some of the white paint on the fender remains. *C. Carter*

Adam Street from 12th July.

The flat fare was raised to 1½*d*. on 5th June, 1949, except on route 16, where it was still 1*d*. The problem of change was worsened, and meant that the P.A.Y.E. was no longer successful, so the decision to end it was made in September 1950. This can be seen to have been a very retrograde step; the system could surely have been further developed to allow the eventual elimination of conductors. But instead the old system of graduated fares came back, with all the costs of administrative clerical staff, inspectors and conductors. P.A.Y.E. ceased on 12th November, 1950.

In Cardiff at this time there were about half-a-dozen people who were unhappy about the closure of the tramways; up to now, each abandonment had passed almost unnoticed, but it is thanks to this small number of enthusiasts, chief among them Ian L. Wright, that the last car to Roath Park was given suitable honours. Wintry gales were blowing on the evening of Saturday, 3rd December, 1949, when a small group of people awaited No. 107's arrival at Roath Park; the car had been decorated by the enthusiasts, and included the words 'Farewell Roath Park' chalked in large lettering on the dash, draped around with festoons of red and green paper streamers, which also decorated the lower-deck windows.

On arrival, the passengers, 'reception committee', driver and conductor were grouped for photographs, taken by the enthusiasts who had ridden from St Mary Street. At 11.10 pm, No. 107 left Ninian Road terminus, with the 'fans' on board, for Roath Depot. It is recorded in the *South Wales Echo* that as the car passed down Ninian Road three people ran out of a house and stood on the pavement, waving flags and quietly cheering. 'The diminishing note of No. 107's bell was borne on the wind at frequent intervals, until she lurched round a corner and was lost to ear and eye.'

Trolleybuses started on this route, which was renumbered 3, on Sunday, 4th December, 1949. Before the abandonment of this tramway, there were 29 tramcars remaining in service; 35 had been scrapped since 1947. Since August 1949, a contractor had been breaking them up at the rear of Roath Depot.

Closure of the final tram route was not long delayed. This was to have been on Saturday, 18th February, 1950, but a last-minute change of plan caused the service to operate for one more day. The last service car was No. 112; before it left St Mary Street at 10.45 pm it had been decorated with coloured ribbons and chalked messages: on the front, 'Going but not forgotten', and on the side, 'Well done old timer'.

The car was very crowded, and Light Railway Transport League members from London, Birmingham and Manchester were on board. Traffic Inspector L.H. Childs, who had more than 30 years' service with the Tramways, drove No. 112 as far as City Road/Albany Road junction; and Driver A. White took over for the final stage to Whitchurch Road terminus.

From here it returned to Roath Depot, the only passengers on arrival being transport employees, a reporter, and the LRTL members. Arrival at the depot was at 11.30 pm.

Trolley buses took over Service l on Monday, 20th February, 1950; but during the whole of that day a specially-decorated car, No. 11, ran between St Mary

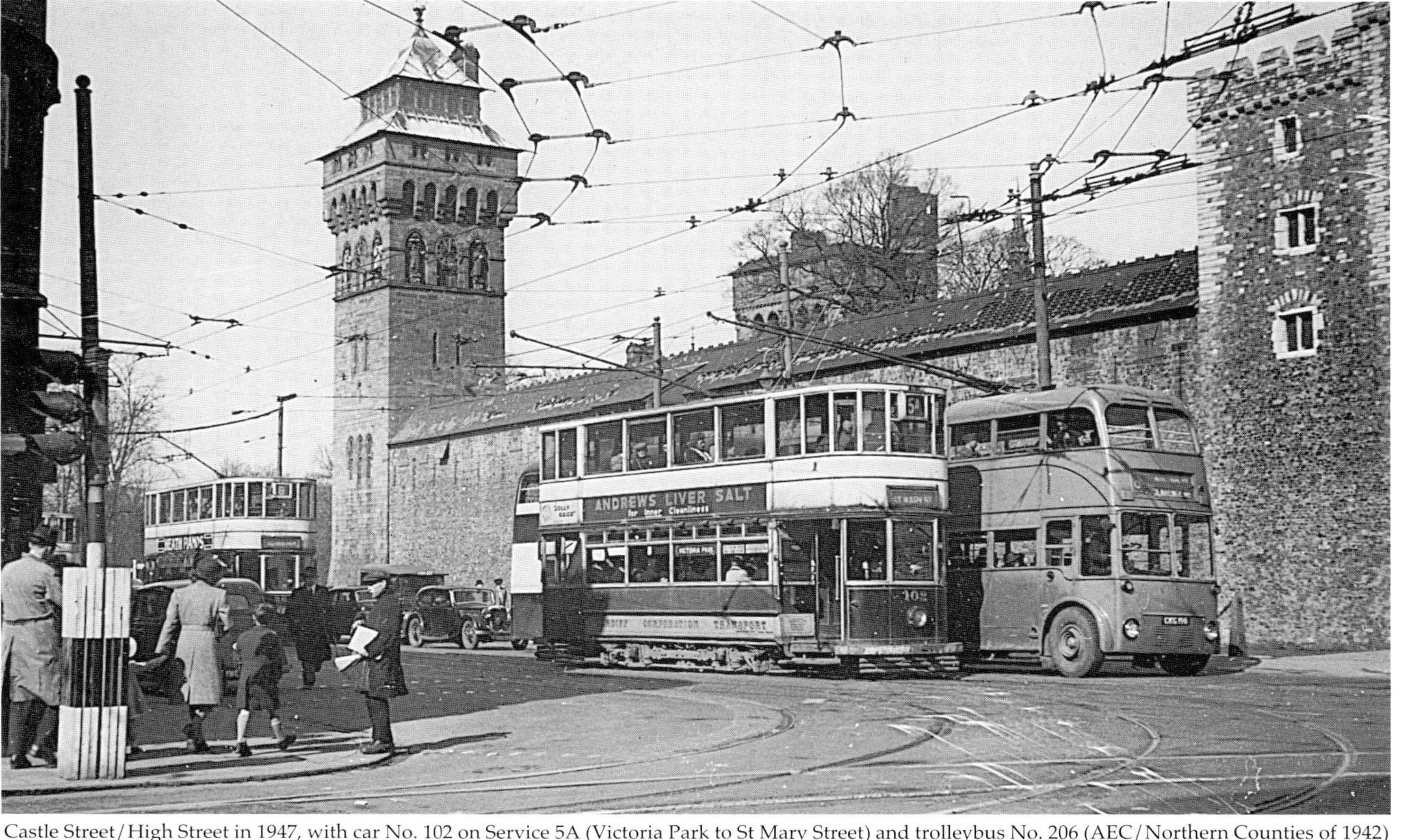

Castle Street/High Street in 1947, with car No. 102 on Service 5A (Victoria Park to St Mary Street) and trolleybus No. 206 (AEC/Northern Counties of 1942) working Service 6 from Cathedral Road to Clarence Road. Both vehicles are about to turn into High Street; note the separate wiring for trams and trolleybuses.

Albany Road junction, a convergence of five roads and the point where the Roath Park trams parted company with those bound for Whitchurch Road. Car No. 4 on Service 1A comes off Crwys Road and enters City Road on 10th February, 1949. *Ian L. Wright*

The passing-loop in Whitchurch Road opposite Maitland Street as seen from the photographer's house. Since the October 1948 derailment the road has been patched up. Car No. 39 on Service 1B to St Mary Street via Duke Street passes No. 83 bound for Whitchurch Road terminus, seen in the distance, in May 1949. See page 133. *Ian L Wright*

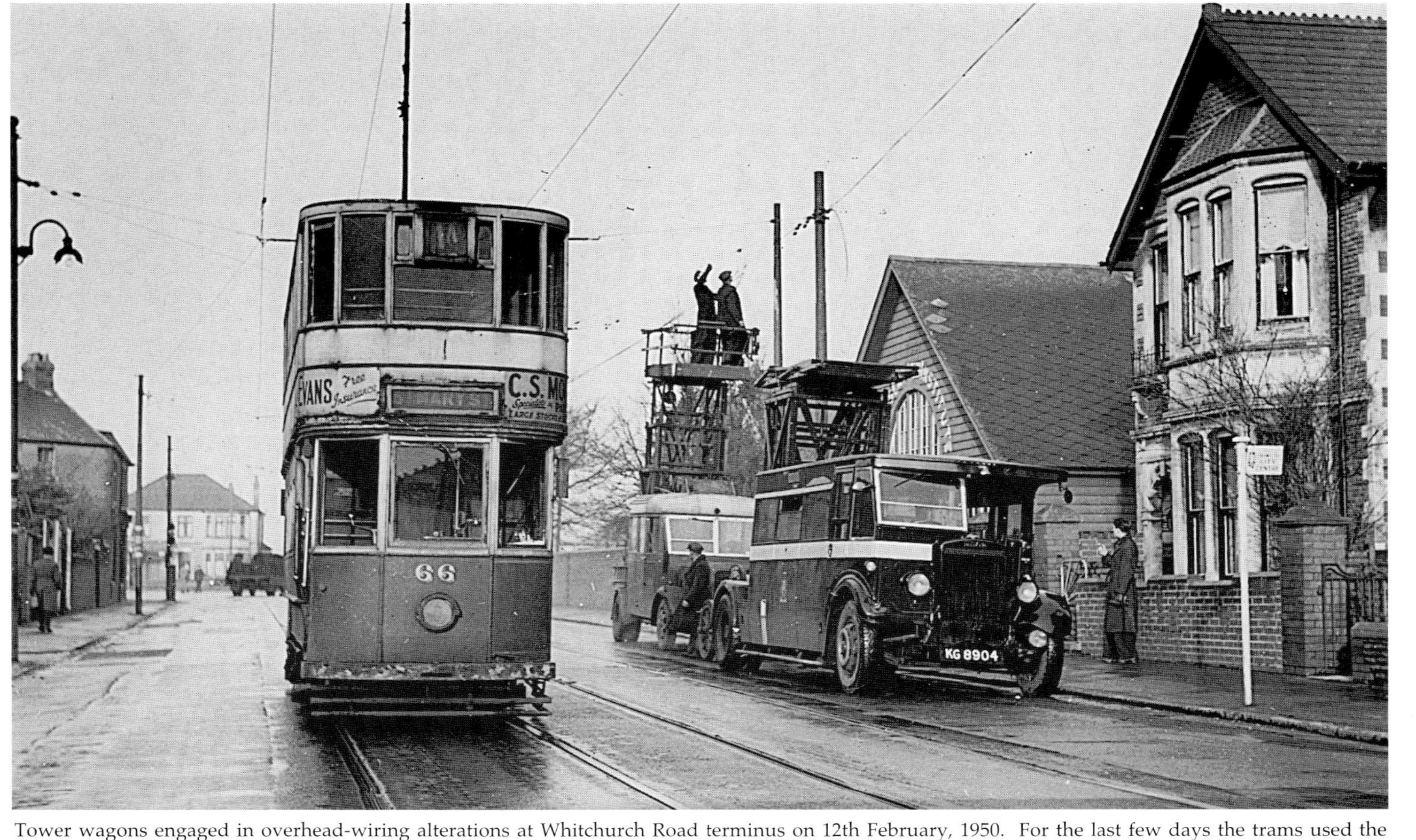

Tower wagons engaged in overhead-wiring alterations at Whitchurch Road terminus on 12th February, 1950. For the last few days the trams used the positive wire of the trolleybus overhead.

Ian L. Wright

Car No. 67 on service 4a to Roath Park drops down to pass beneath the Queen Street railway bridges; later the road was to be even more lowered. Both track and paving were in very poor state when this picture was taken on 19th March, 1949. *Ian L. Wright*

From 12th July, 1949, surviving tram services were diverted via Adam Street. Here on 8th November, 1949, is car No. 20 from Whitchurch Road to St Mary Street in Glossop Road about to turn into Moira Terrace; in the foreground are the abandoned tracks to Adamsdown Square. *Ian L. Wright*

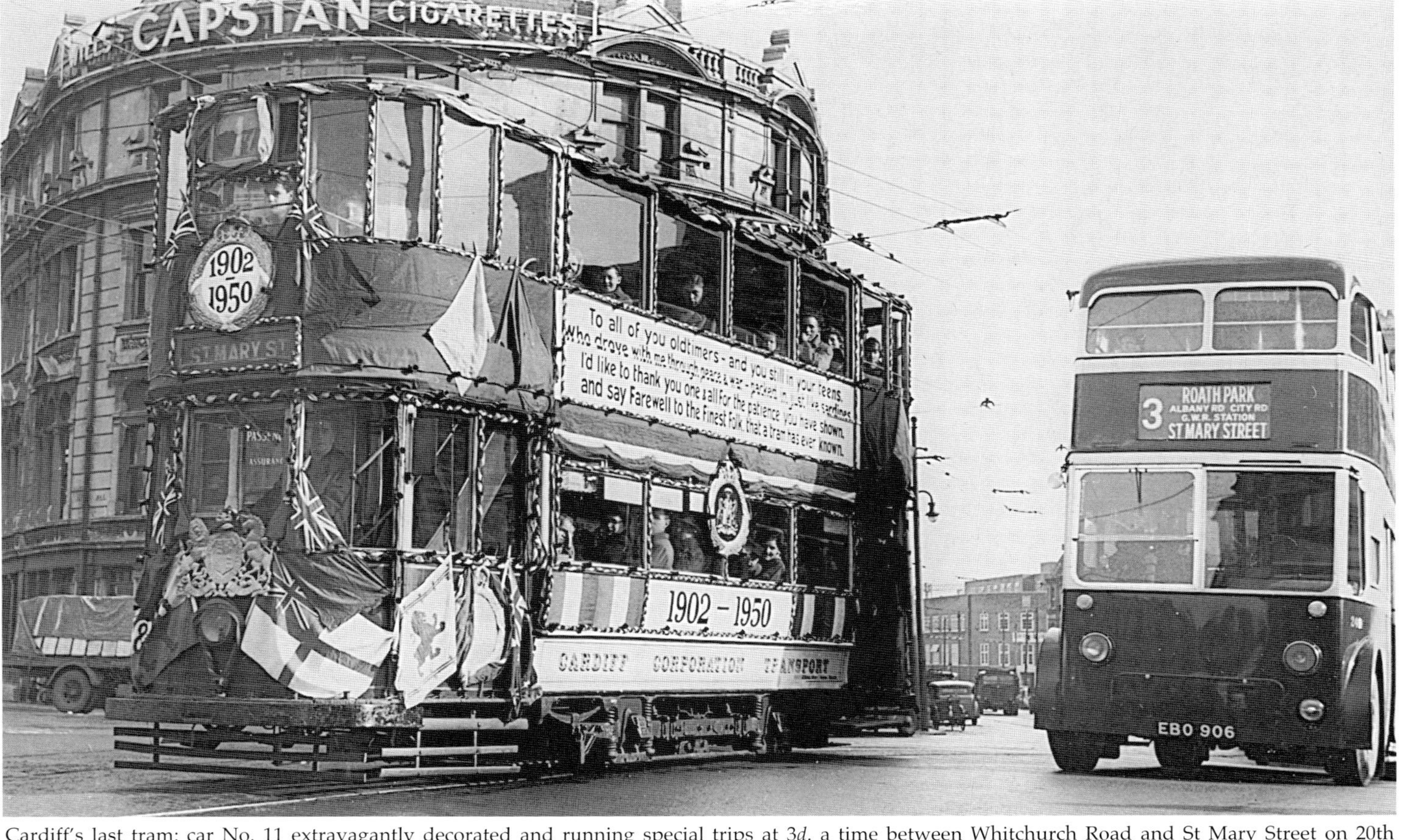

Cardiff's last tram: car No. 11 extravagantly decorated and running special trips at *3d.* a time between Whitchurch Road and St Mary Street on 20th February, 1950. It is here shown turning from Custom House Street into St Mary Street alongside trolleybus No. 249 (BUT/East Lancs). *Ian L. Wright*

Street and Whitchurch Road. Passengers wishing to ride on this had to pay 3*d*. for the privilege, and special souvenir tickets were issued, with the wording 'Souvenir Ticket. 3*d*. 1902 to 1950. Service No. 1 - St Mary Street & Whitchurch Road.' The car was crowded on most trips, and by the evening the demand for rides was so great that a relief car (No. 112) had to be brought out running just ahead of No. 11. In the evening, the decorated car was a blaze of light.

And so the time came for the final journey from Whitchurch Road to the depot. On board were the Lord Mayor, Alderman T.J. Kerrigan; members of the City Council; and some of the people who had been connected with the tramways over their 48 years. Shouting, rattle-waving, bell-ringing crowds surging against the car brought it to a stand many times during that journey, which took an hour for the 2½ miles.

It was an occasion for sentiment and reminiscence.

> Tonight we feel we are parting with an old friend, *said the Lord Mayor*. The thrill of those early days will provide childhood memories which will always remain. The last bell has been rung, the last ticket issued, and we can only hope the modern successors may prove as reliable and serve us with as fine a record as the departed.

Then he presented Councillor Pat Collins, Chairman of the transport department, with a brass bell from the tram. Two of the oldest serving drivers received a chromium-plated control key each from Mr J.F. Siddall, now General Manager. Two long-serving conductors were congratulated by the Lord Mayor.

The coloured lights of the tram were extinguished shortly before it arrived at the depot, but came on again for the last few yards, as it slowly moved past the long line of redundant tramcars, followed by pipers and drummers of the 42nd Scots Battalion Boy Scout band.

So that was it. Unbelievable as it must seem today, a financially successful tramway system had been scrapped, merely because it was thought that trams were 'old-fashioned'. The cars themselves were burnt at the back of Roath depot during April 1950, all useful fittings having been removed; and the remains are lying there to this day, underneath a mass of concrete.

Little survived of the tramway era. Roath Depot continued in use for many years, first for trolley buses then for motor buses. Of the four front entrances three were bricked up and the extreme eastern one was enlarged. Alongside the south-west wall a single length of tramway track, laid in granite setts and with track drains marked 'Hadfield Patent Sheffield', was left in place, and there were more tracks inside the depot. On 24th September, 1986, Roath Depot was declared closed by the Lord Mayor, Councillor David Myfyr Evans, who in his short speech referred to 'this place of history and memories' and the building was soon demolished.

None of the interesting top-covered cars was saved, as in those days there was neither the money nor the inclination to preserve anything old, as there is today. Nor had the transport committee any intention of officially preserving a car, the impression being that it wished to forget that it had ever operated trams!

Electric street transport remained in Cardiff for another 20 years until

Sunday, 11th January, 1970, when the last trolley bus was run; thus the transport committee, who had never wanted to operate trolley buses in the first place, finally got its own way.

Soon afterwards the long-established route pattern was altered, and during 1974/5 the handsome and dignified maroon and cream livery was replaced by a harsh orange and white, and the city's proper coat of arms was replaced, on the buses, by a simplified version, without motto. Services became so infrequent that roadside timetables were posted in many places - something never deemed necessary in tram and trolley bus days. One-man operation of buses was introduced between 1970 and 1980, and the buses carried boards proclaiming 'Exact Fare Only' - but no information was provided at bus stops to tell intending passengers what that fare might be, and drivers were not prepared to give change. However, it was possible to buy from information points a season ticket that gave unlimited travel on trains and buses within the Cardiff area.

It is to be hoped that a city of this size and importance will once again enjoy the benefits of electric rail transport, in some shape or form, and that its return will not be too long delayed.

Last day on Service 1, and Light Railway Transport League members are seen on the top deck of car No. 28 at Whitchurch Road, 19th February, 1950. *Left to right*: Geoffrey Booth, Owen Prosser, P.F. Roberts, Derek Chaplin, Eric Old, tramwayman, Miss Booth, tramwayman, Gwen Booth, - Penrose, Ted Collins, and Robert Jones. *Ian L. Wright*

Chapter Eleven

Track Renewal

One of the features of electrically-worked tramways which may have helped to bring them into disfavour was the frightening speed with which the rails became worn, and the enormous expense of renewing them. This was certainly the case in Cardiff; indeed, only two years after opening, some interlaced track in Newport Road was needing heavy repairs owing to soft and wet subsoil under the concrete along the sewer trench.

Then again, the curse of corrugations, which caused the Committee much distress, was rife. In September 1905 the manager recommended the purchase of a railgrinder, as the rails in some places were already very badly corrugated. By September 1906 the single-line section in Cowbridge Road, between Llandaff Road and Clive Road, was 'in a bad state of repair' and doubling this section was recommended.

The situation was getting desperate. In May 1907 Mr Ellis reported on the condition of the track. Corrugations had increased tenfold and the railgrinder was unable to cope with them. The worst sections were in Cowbridge Road and Ninian Road where there were single or interlaced lines; and in Bute Street and Queen Street where traffic was heavy and service speed was greatest. Features such as these were thought to be most likely to cause corrugations, but the manager had been doing some research and had noted that the various railways that operated steam rail motor trains also suffered from corrugated track, while those that did not had none. He therefore concluded that it was a defect in the design of the motor train, or electric tram, that caused them. The trouble was unknown in horse-tram days. No remedy could be found, so all that could be done was to replace completely the worst sections, and from Hadfields of Sheffield 200 yards run of single track at 15*s.* 3*d.* a yard, plus two sets of crossover points and crossings at £204 10*s.*, were purchased.

In April 1908 track repairs in City Road and Cowbridge Road were required, the estimated cost to be £850 and £800 respectively. As the portion of City Road needing attention was in a very bad state, and with a prospect of heavy summer traffic, this was done first.

During the 1900s there was a continuous programme of minor repairs, but by 1915 about a quarter of the track had been completely renewed, and opportunity was taken to double certain sections, for example Ninian Road, where a new up line was laid to make double track (1st December, 1914). A massive track renewal programme was undertaken, as follows: 1915: The Hayes to City Road. 1915, 1916, 1921-2: Cowbridge Road. 1916, 1920, 1921-2: Bute Street. 1920, 1921: High Street and St Mary Street. 1920: Bute Terrace. 1921: Custom House Street. 1921: Penarth Road. 1921-2: Windsor Place to Crwys Road, Clive Street, Wellfield Road, City Road, Portmanmoor Road, Moira Place, Wood Street junction to Clare Road, Corporation Road, and Castle Street. Special work (1920): new layout City Road and Albany Road junction; new layout at Cathedral Road junction. The following works were in progress

Layout of Osborn's 'Titan' manganese steel for the depot entrance for the Cardiff Corporation Tramways. Taken from an advertisement by the Titan Trackwork Co. Ltd, Sheffield. *John Gillham Collection*

during July 1922: Albany Road; Woodville Road junction-Whitchurch Road; Constellation Street and Tin Street; and Roath Depot. The City Engineer was instructed to proceed with further track reconstruction in Clare Road, costing £12,158; Glossop Road, £4,972; and Meteor Street, £1,840.

When the City Engineer made his report in July 1922 it was in reproving tones, since much of the work had had to be put off because of the War.

> This was unfortunate, not only because for some years large sums of money had to be expended upon the temporary patching, but because during that period the track rapidly became worse, rendering total reconstruction essential, whereas if the work could have been carried out at the proper time, it would have been much less extensive.

Opportunity was taken to replace the centre poles supporting the overhead with side poles and span wire in such places as Ninian Road and Cathedral Road; for the latter, unemployed labourers were used. When the Salisbury Road line was relaid, the entire section was closed, and cars worked via City Road. This was exceptional; the normal method was to have single-line working with temporary crossovers. By February 1923 the programme was nearly completed, only two further sections requiring complete reconstruction - Mill Lane, and the original single track in Ninian Road.

During July 1923 Clarence Bridge needed repairs and was closed for a fortnight. Presumably the Clarence Road services had to terminate just short of the bridge.

A 'Celerity' railgrinding machine was purchased from The Equipment & Engineering Co. for £569; armed with this, the Tramways Committee felt certain that the new track would have a long life.

In October 1925 it was proposed to alter the layout of City Road Junction; in June 1926 the tender of Hadfields at £2,646 for the work was accepted; and the work was carried out in April 1927. The junction as originally installed had been very unsatisfactory as it was mainly single track. For instance, a car from City Road turning right into Newport Road had first to enter a single-line section at the bottom of City Road, run on the wrong side of the road, then round the corner and along Newport Road for some way, still on the wrong side, before crossing over to the correct side. Similarly, a car from Glossop Road had to cross right over Newport Road, then get to the correct side by means of the same crossover. This crazy junction was presided over by a pointsman who would hold up a red disc for a city-bound car in City Road until Newport Road was clear, then turn the disc to white. By 1913 some improvement had been made and there were double-line connections from City Road into Newport Road and from Glossop Road into Newport Road. In the 1927 reconstruction a double-line direct from City Road to Glossop Road replaced the single-line connection. However the eastern side of the junction was unaltered (*see maps on page 38*).

In 1930 Hadfields supplied rails, points and crossings for the Bute Street, Bute Terrace and Custom House Street junctions for £3,349. The reconstruction of Cardiff Bridge necessitated single-line working in the outward direction only. Inward journeys were diverted via Lower Cathedral Road or Neville Street, and

thence via Tudor street and Wood Street.

What was virtually the last track improvement came late in 1935, when in conjunction with the widening of Newport Road near Roath Court the section of single-track was doubled, the Ministry of Transport having consented to this in September 1935. From now on, any track in bad condition was not renewed, but allowed to get into such a state that sound argument could be made for scrapping the tramways. Nevertheless, late in 1936 the Duke Street, Castle Street and High Street junction was reconstructed at a cost of £2,235.

But now the whole of the older track in Cathedral Road, from the junction to fifty yards beyond Sneyd Street, was in a very bad condition and urgently needing repair, it being beyond patching up. Nothing was done; again in October 1937 the City Engineer stated that the track and woodpaving were getting worse and there had been complaints from the public about excessive noise. It was resolved to put the track in a reasonable state of repair for three years, because the Royal Agricultural Show was to be held at Pontcanna Farm in 1938, and the traffic could be carried more expeditiously by tram. Even so, nothing had been done to the track by June 1938, and it seems unlikely that anything was done until its closure.

The old loop at Roath Park terminus was worn out by November 1937 and, as its replacement cost would be high, the manager recommended its removal and a relay of the points and crossover.

Over the years, the various track renewals and improvements had eliminated many single-track sections, and most of the routes were now in wide, straight streets with continuous lengths of double track. However, in 1939 there were still two single-line sections in Cowbridge Road, two at the north end of Whitchurch Road, one in Meteor Street, one in Hayes Bridge, and interlaced track across Clarence Bridge. These were to last right up to their closure, as no money would now be spent on tramway improvements.

Incidentally, for all new track used after about 1915, B.S. No. 4 rails in 60 ft lengths were employed.

The track in Cowbridge Road was so bad by 1947 that a 12 mph speed restriction was imposed on trams after an accident on 10th April that year, when No. 112 left the rails and hit a shop window.

Chapter Twelve

Depots and Power Station

The main car shed of the system was at Roath, and included the car overhaul works. The depot was a very fine structure, although somewhat dwarfed by the adjacent power station.

Four tracks led into the front of the depot by means of arched doorways, and each of these tracks branched into three; thus there were twelve roads inside the shed, with a capacity of 100 tramcars. The four bays were each 320 ft long with a total width of 136 ft. About two-thirds of the way into the shed was an electric traverser to shunt cars from one track to another, or to the repair shops beyond, which occupied the remaining one-third of the building.

These included a capacious machine shop; a paint shop; a smithy; a carpenters' shop; and messroom, oil, and sand stores. The foremen's office, between the paint and machine shops, commanded a view of the whole interior.

After the trolley buses had vanished and then until the 1980s Roath Depot was the main repair works for Cardiff buses, and even in 1974 they were still hand-painted, not sprayed. Inside the depot the tramway 'atmosphere' remained strong, as the tracks were still there; in places the floor was paved with the original wood blocks, and there were other reminders of the trams, such as a ventilator scoop which was used to open paint tins! By 1974 the old city power station had been demolished and on 24th September, 1986, the depot was closed, superseded by a new depot and repair works at Sloper Road, Leckwith, which also replaced the long-established bus garage and repair shops at Sloper Road.

Roath shedded the cars working the Eastern routes of the city; for the Western routes a smaller shed at Clare Road was provided; this held 32 trams, and had a 'family likeness' to Roath, both having been erected at the same time, by Messrs D.W. Davies. In 1923 the entry to Clare Road depot was altered to allow cars to run in from the south instead of the north; extensions and alterations were carried out by S.C. Taverner of Newport three years later. Further special trackwork was supplied by the Titan Trackwork Co. of Sheffield, for this depot.

Clare Road was converted to a trolley bus depot in 1942 and closed to trams on 25th August, 1946. It ceased to be used as a depot in 1953, but still existed in the 1980s as the City Health Department vehicle workshops.

A former horse-car depot at Wood Street was re-equipped to contain about 10 single-deck trams on 31st March, 1904; it was swept away when Wood Street was redeveloped in the late 'thirties. Other horse-car depots, at Severn Road and Cathays, were not re-used.

An unusual feature was that for many years the section of track in Newport Road between Broadway and Roath Depot was not used by service cars, presumably because that part of the road had not yet become built up; service 2A was extended to the depot on 20th August, 1927, and later service 2 was similarly extended. Another feature was that passengers could ride on cars travelling to and from the depot, even 'off-route' journeys, in which case one could observe almost all the service numbers in Cardiff on cars in Newport Road.

A peep inside Roath depot shows no fewer than nine of the Brush-built single-deck trams, plus one covered-top, two open-top and the railcleaning car, No. 131 (number not carried).

Author's Collection

ROATH DEPOT AND POWER STATION

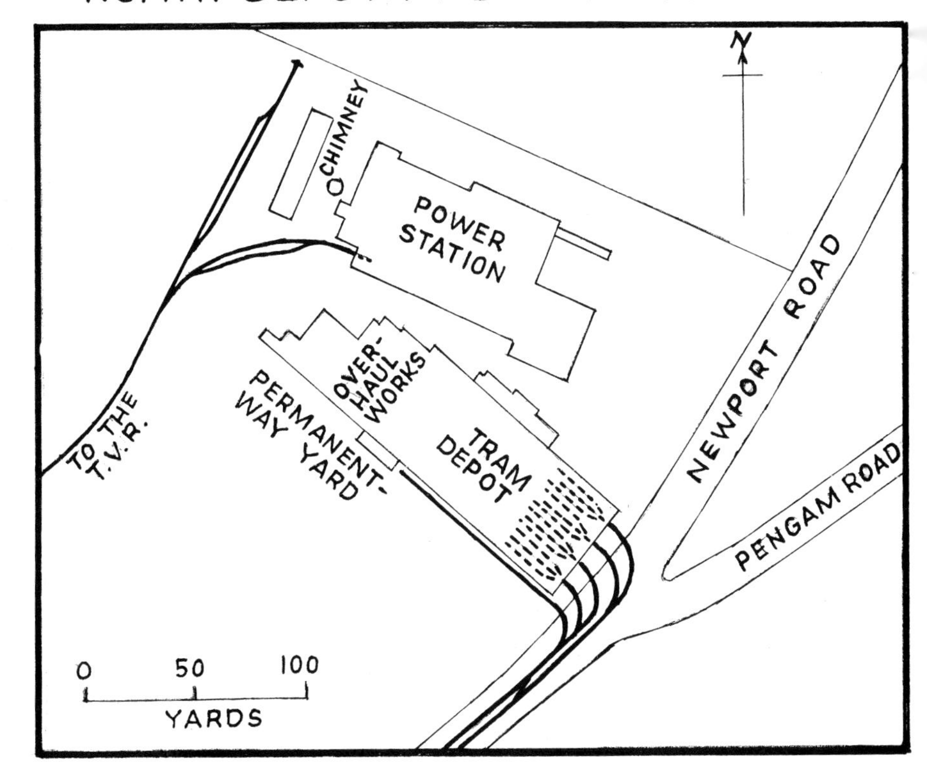

A 1927-built single-deck car No. 117 at Roath depot on 7th January, 1936; in October of that year the Splott-Grangetown service would be closed and the cars put into store. *H.B. Priestley*

Roath depot, 7th January, 1937. Stored single-deck cars Nos. 44 and 135 of 1926/7, double-deck car No. 10, and a single-deck bus (BO 5225). *H.B. Priestley*

The Tramways Department also owned its own power station, close alongside Roath depot. Originally, it had 16 Musgrave Lancashire boilers at 150 lb. pressure, with Musgrave superheaters and two 288-tube Green's economisers. There were four 500 hp and four 1600 hp Musgrave steam engines of the inverted vertical cross-compound condensing type, with a flywheel and generator between the high- and low-pressure sides.

These engines drove four Westinghouse compound-wound 8-pole DC 500-550 volt generators of 300 kw capacity, also two 1000 kw Dick, Kerr generators and two 1100 kw GEC three-phase generators. There were also two Bruce Peebles 80 kw motor-generators with a Tudor battery of 56 cells, and a Westinghouse switchboard, which by 1908 was giving a total capacity of 5,560 kw. This was far more than necessary for the tramways alone, but the Tramways Department sold a bulk supply of current to the Corporation Lighting Department, augmenting the output of the Lighting Department's own power station which had been opened in December 1894.

By 1913 another four smaller motor-generator sets had been added, bringing the total capacity up to 7,000 kw, and there was also one 2,500 KVA Willans-Siemens turbo-alternator. By 1921 there were 10 motor-generators of seven different types, which brought the total capacity up to 14,400 kw, of which 12,000 kw was available for bulk supply to the Lighting Department. Presumably the tramways managed on only 2,400 kw. By now there had also been added four Babcock boilers to augment the 16 original ones. During 1920-21 the Tramways Department received £72,650 from the Lighting Department for the bulk sale of electricity.

As from 31st March, 1923, the Tramways Power Station was transferred to the Electricity Supply Department, whose own combined total output now grew to 32,800 kw, of which 3,350 kw remained available for the Tramways Department for at least the next sixteen years and probably more.

(The above notes on the power supply were contributed by John Gillham.)

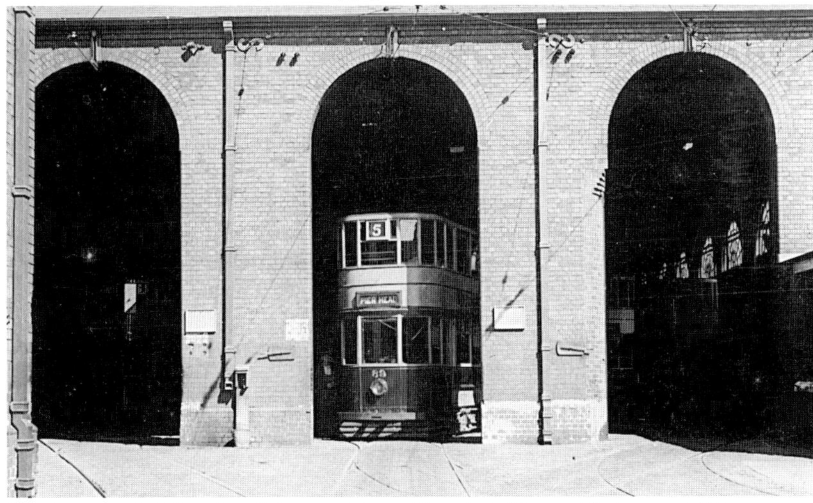

The forecourt of Clare Road depot, with car No. 89 visible, on 8th August, 1939.

H.B. Priestley

Chapter Thirteen

Tramcars

The 'first generation' of electric tramcars in Cardiff comprised 130 passenger vehicles and one rail-cleaning car. First order was placed with the Electric Railway and Tramway Carriage Works Ltd. (Dick, Kerr), of Preston, on 12th August, 1901, for 54 trams of three types. Delivery of these was much delayed, since at the time dozens of other towns were also ordering tramcars.

Nos. 1-20 were four-wheel open-top double-deck cars, each having three windows a side, and cost £540 each. Each vehicle had a Brill 21E truck, the spring base of which was 14 ft 6 in. and the extreme length of the top plate 15 ft 7 in. The wheels, which were 30 in. in diameter, had steel tyres with wrought iron centres, and were made by John Baker & Co., Rotherham. Wheelbase was 6 ft. The car itself measured 28 ft 6 in. over fenders, the platforms being 5 ft 9 in. and internal length 16 ft. Owing to some of Cardiff's railway bridges imposing a maximum height of 15 ft from rail to trolley joint, the internal headroom of the car was only 6 ft, the overall height from rail to trolley plank, on the top-deck floor, being 9 ft. Seating capacity was 30 on the top deck and 22 inside.

Nos. 21-40 were very handsome bogie cars, which were more capacious than the small 4-wheelers, and had four windows each side. The bogies were of the maximum-traction type, with driving wheels 30 in. and pony wheels 20 in. in diameter; the bogie had a wheelbase of 4 ft and was of the Brill '22E' type. Length over fenders was 34 ft 6 in. and inside length 21 ft 4 in., the platform being 5 ft 9 in. Vertical dimensions were the same as those of the 4-wheelers. Seating capacity was 38 upstairs and 30 inside; the cost of each of these trams was £650.

Nos. 41-54 were single-deck cars to work the Salisbury Road line; the bogies were the same as for Nos. 21-40. Overall length of the car was 33 ft 6 in., interior length 24 ft 4 in., while the platform was only 3 ft 9 in. Seating capacity was 34 and there were two compartments.

Features common to all the double-deck cars will now be described. They were designed to the general specification of Arthur Ellis, who clearly must have favoured straight stairways with landing half-way up, which they all had instead of the far more common twisting stairs. All had Tidswell life-guards and fenders. Inside were longitudinal seats of lath and space, with 'garden seats' upstairs. The car windows were draped with neat red curtains with the initials 'CCT' worked on each one; this certainly gave the tram an air of opulence. Interior finish consisted of light and dark oak, with ceilings of three-ply bird's-eye maple divided into panels by oak mouldings. All had Dick, Kerr electrical equipment, comprising two DK 25A motors and two DB 1 Form B controllers per car.

On 12th May, 1902, another 40 cars were ordered from the same manufacturers: 20 4-wheel cars, Nos. 55-74, to the same design as Nos. 1-20; and 20 more bogie cars, Nos. 75-94, similar to Nos. 21-40. Prices for the respective

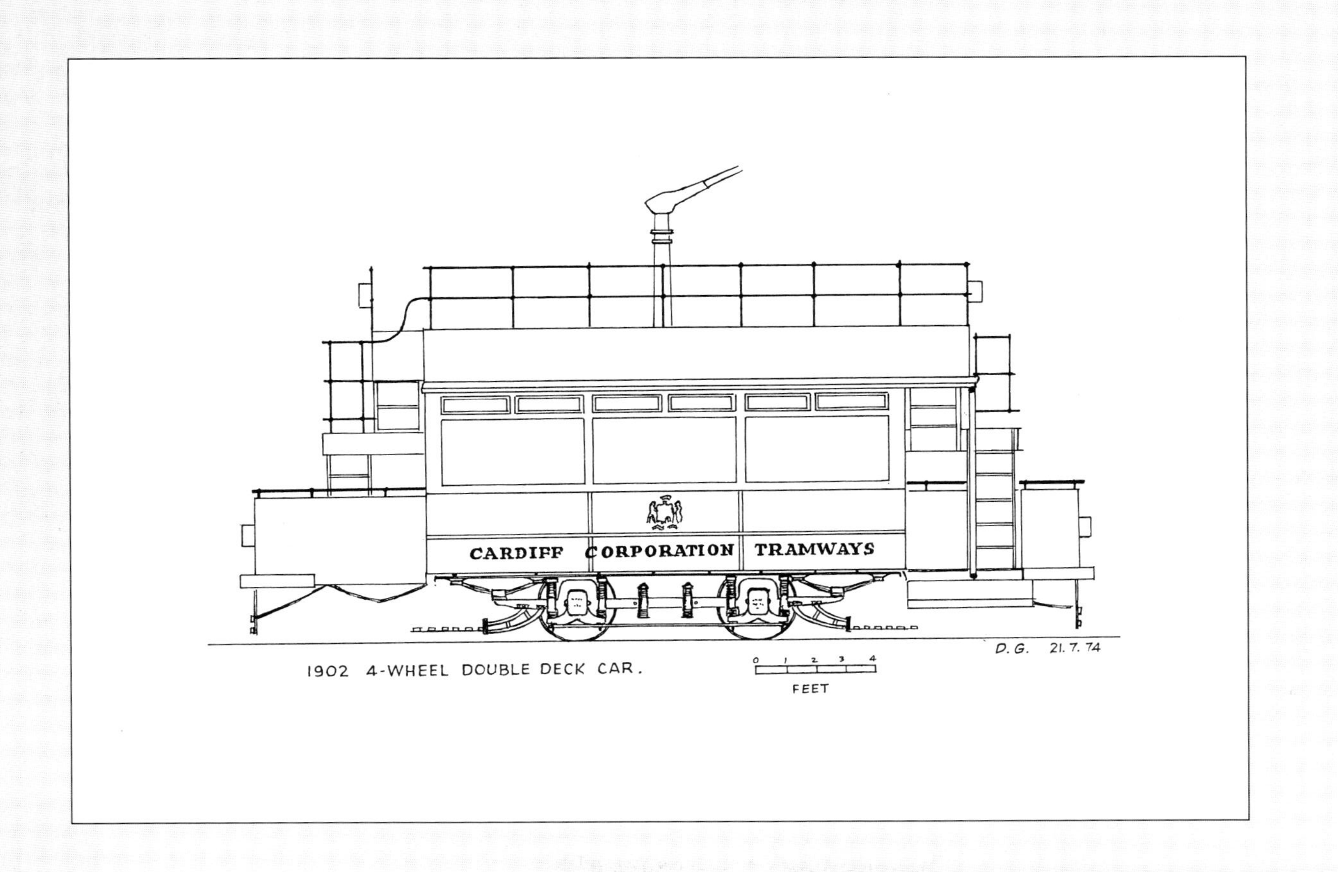

1902 4-WHEEL DOUBLE DECK CAR.

One of the 1902-built bogie cars (Nos. 21-40) at an unidentified location, photographed when new. *D.W.K. Jones Collection*

types were the same. One 1,000 gallon rail-cleaning car had also been ordered from Dick, Kerr, on the 11th February, 1902 (*see Chapter 14*).

By 1903 the tramcar market had become very competitive, with prices of new cars being reduced; thus in February of that year the British Thomson-Houston Co. successfully tendered for the supply of twenty 4-wheel double-deck cars, similar to those already running, for only £504 each. Dimensions were the same as the Dick, Kerr cars; but BTH sub-contracted the work of body construction to the Brush Electrical Engineering Co., who received the order in June, and BTH supplied the equipment only: chief of which was two GE58 28 hp motors and B18 controllers per car. The usual Brill 21E 6 ft wheelbase truck was fitted; the cars were numbered 95 to 114, and apparently were rather slow-running, compared to the earlier cars. They were delivered early in 1904.

Further single-deck cars were now required for the Splott-Grangetown route, which was temporarily being worked by some of the double-deck cars cut down to single deck. An experimental single-deck car, with 36 seats, including 18 for smokers, was ordered from British Thomson-Houston, who sub-contracted the work of body construction to G.F. Milnes & Co., Ltd, Hadley, Shropshire. The car, which had Brill 22E 4 ft wheelbase maximum-traction trucks, was 36 ft long with open platforms, and the end windows could be opened. This car, No. 115, was presumably successful, for fifteen more were ordered in December 1903, this time from the British Westinghouse Electric Co. Ltd, who supplied the electrical equipment. The bodies were built by Milnes at their Hadley works, under sub-contract from Westinghouse, and the cars had Brush 4 ft maximum-traction bogies. Overall length of the cars was 37 ft 6 in. over fenders, the internal length being 16 ft. The greater part of each platform was given over to smoking compartments, each seating five passengers, the platforms being open-ended, as with the prototype car. Total seating capacity was 40, four higher than the prototype. These vehicles cost £601 10s. each, and all had arrived by July 1904; numbers were 116 to 130. All orders were now fulfilled.

Over the years, modifications were made to some members of the fleet: some cars that had been reduced to single-deckers were restored to original condition after the arrival of the Splott single-deck bogie cars, with the exception of No. 3, which was kept as a ticket and parcels car until the 'twenties. In 1914 single-deck car No. 44 was vestibuled and bogie car No. 30 was fitted with new GE200K motors and BTH B49 controllers. All cars were fitted with illuminated destination indicators, made by the British Electric Car Company, and, on Ellis's recommendation, they were also equipped with service number indicators. New BTH equipment, similar to that on No. 30, was later fitted to Nos. 26, 33, 36, 75, 80, 82, 83, 85 and 86. Single-deck trams 116, 117 and 127 received new BTH B510A controllers; whilst No. 98 lost its original BTH equipment in favour of Dick, Kerr. Nos. 12, 15 and 98 had their 'broken' stairways replaced by conventional curved ones. Miscellaneous equipment ordered from time to time included two Dick, Kerr 10 A3 motors, on 4th November, 1913, and one set of mechanical track brakes from Hurst Nelson & Co. Ltd of Motherwell in 1919, for the 21E truck of the scrubber car. This car (131) was converted to a railgrinder in 1920; the track-brake gear pressed carborundum blocks on to the track, while

water gushed from the tank.

In 1921, the department staff at Roath shops rebuilt one bogie car, No. 24, with extended canopies, curved stairways, and enlarged and enclosed platforms. Instead of a round dash, an angular one was fitted. Seating capacity was increased by ten to 78; Nos. 22, 23, 29, 30, 32, 34, 76, 84 and 90 were similarly altered in 1922. All ten were given new GE200K motors and B49 controllers. Six of the single-deck cars received vestibules in 1923: Nos. 42, 43, 45, 48, 115 and 125, the last two of which in addition were given BTH GE200K motors with B510 controllers. Four-wheel cars 5, 6, 10, 13, 72 and 99 were given new Peckham Pendulum P22 trucks, retaining Dick, Kerr equipment, and the top-deck seating was increased to 38, vestibules and canopies being fitted. The rebuilds were completed during 1922.

However, what was really needed was a fleet of modern, totally-enclosed double-deck tramcars. The big problem was that normal-height cars would be unable to pass under the railway bridges, with their 15 ft headroom. The Brush Company had recently patented a type of lowbridge car with small wheels and motors; and in November 1922 Mr Horsfield was instructed to purchase a sample car at a cost of £ 1,735.

The Brush Electrical Engineering Co. Ltd constructed the body (which had 24 lower-deck and 40 top-deck seats) and the special well-type underframe with its floor much lower than usual. The Peckham Truck & Engineering Company Ltd supplied a four-wheeled Patent Pendulum P22 truck, of 7 ft 6 in. wheelbase, with wheels only 26 in. in diameter; its special feature being a flexible suspension on the axleboxes to give smoother running on straight track and enabling the car to take curves well. Lastly, the British Thomson-Houston Company supplied electrical equipment: two 35/40 hp GE265 special small and light motors, and two B510A controllers of a new design. In addition to the driving and reversing levers, these controllers incorporated a third spindle projecting through the top; by placing the reversing handle on this spindle, the motorman could cut either motor out of circuit at will - a useful facility for electrical fault-finding. Electric braking was simplified by the facility of being able to stop the car merely by moving the controller handle to the brake notches, whether the car was travelling forwards or backwards; and the electric braking worked even if one motor was out of circuit. A fan inside each motor kept it cool.

The component parts duly arrived in Cardiff, and were transferred from the GWR's Roath Branch siding to Roath Depot and assembled. On 26th March, 1923, the Tramways Committee went to the depot, inspected the car (No. 101) and went on a trial run to Pier Head and back. The members were obviously very pleased with the car, for they accepted the General Manager's recommendation to purchase 25 more at an estimated cost of £43,350, the sum to be borrowed from the Ministry of Transport. Brush supplied the bodies, at £915 each; BTH the equipment, at £476 12*s*. for each car; and Peckham supplied 25 more of their trucks at £183 each.

Nine new cars had been delivered by 14th December, 1923, and were put into service that evening; the remainder came the following January. They took the numbers of old cars, which were sold to scrap merchants, and not in any

Car No. 30, one of the bogie cars of 1902, as fitted with BTH controllers and rebuilt with enclosed platforms, curved stairways and extended canopies in 1921. It is on service 2A (Victoria Park to Newport Road), standing outside Roath depot. *Author's Collection*

A 1904-built single-deck car with Milnes body, one of two vestibuled in the early 1920s, specially posed for the photographer at Clare Road depot on 10th July, 1938. Seats for smokers were at each end. *W.A. Camwell*

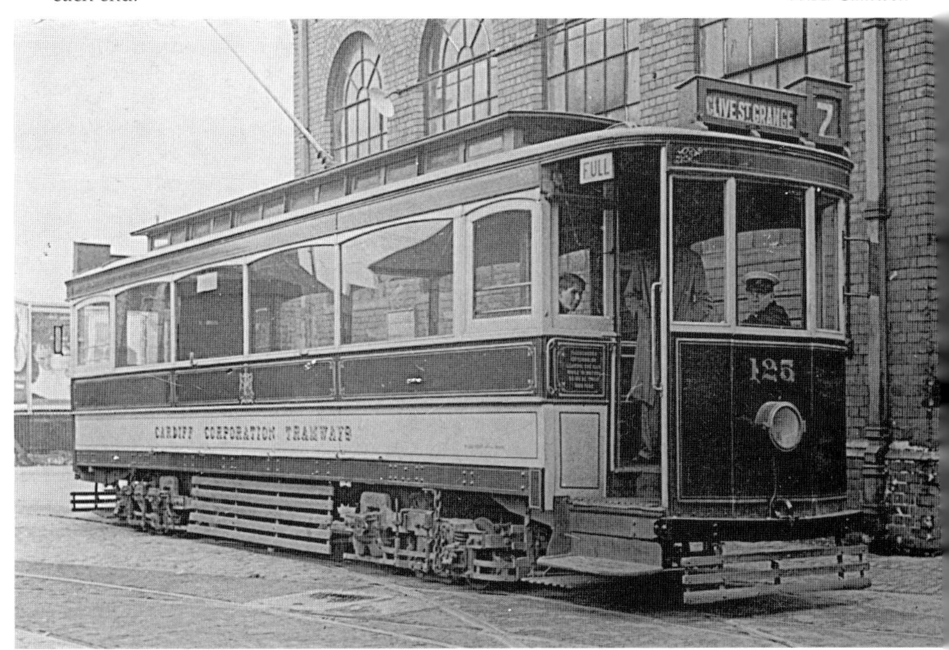

particular order: Nos. 2, 9, 20, 56, 57, 62, 66, 70, 95-97, 100, 102-114.

The cars were constructed to the very high standard of workmanship customary in those days. The lower-saloon interior was finished in oak, with millboard ceiling finished in white enamel. The lower-deck ventilators were designed to allow fresh air to enter at the front end of the car, and stale air to be extracted from the rear end of the saloon. Seating followed the traditional longitudinal facing arrangement, there being accommodation for 12 passengers each side. The upper deck also had traditional seating, transverse with reversible seat-backs, accommodating 40 passengers. Here, the side walls and ceiling were formed of teak slats 2½ in. wide by 1 in. thick, alternate slats being stained with black japan and varnished. Four windows each side, the frames of which were stained with black japan, could be opened by operating a handle (one each side of the car) which lowered all the windows on one side simultaneously. Handrails were brass.

The entire body framing of the cars was constructed of teak, reinforced by steel plates and sections. Oak and American whitewood were also used. The rounded dash panel was made of sheet metal ⅛ in. thick, with a headlamp mounted centrally, somewhat lower down on the first batch of cars.

Height of the cars was 14 ft 10 in.; overall length 29 ft 6 in.; overhang from centre of axle 11 ft; width over rocker panels 6 ft 1½ in.; width overall 7 ft. Height of lower-deck floor from street was 25 in., and height of the top-deck floor from street was 8 ft 4 in. The trams each weighed 10 tons 4 cwt.

In March 1924 it was agreed to purchase 25 more new cars for £46,625, but there were fears that no four-wheel car, even with an advanced design of truck, could ever ride as well as a bogie car, and that inevitably oscillation of the kind graphically referred to as 'tail-wagging' would occur. Cardiff therefore asked John Ferguson, manager of Glasgow tramways, to investigate the problem. On Thursday, 15th May, 1924, he arranged a rather remarkable test. A top-covered car was run down City Road, after traffic had ceased, at a speed of at least 20 mph[!] trailing a thin stream of coloured liquid arranged to fall directly over the rail. This it did; it followed the line of rails exactly. Later, Ferguson made his report:

> On the whole I am of the opinion that your comparatively flat system and, for the most part, moderate speed, together with the restricted height of your car, the fairly long wheelbase of your trucks, and the frequent inspection and overhaul of rolling stock and permanent way, place you in a very comfortable position in regard to oscillation. It may occur in patches, but should never become general.

Apparently the motormen had not yet become used to these new cars, being unaware that the brakes were more powerful than those of the old stock; and they were making unnecessarily savage brake applications, causing wheel-lock and thus flats and excessive noise, about which there had been complaints. Ferguson reported on this, and the matter was put right. The Committee thanked him for his services, paid him for his trouble, and he returned to Glasgow.

Orders were therefore placed in July 1924 with Brush for 25 top-covered

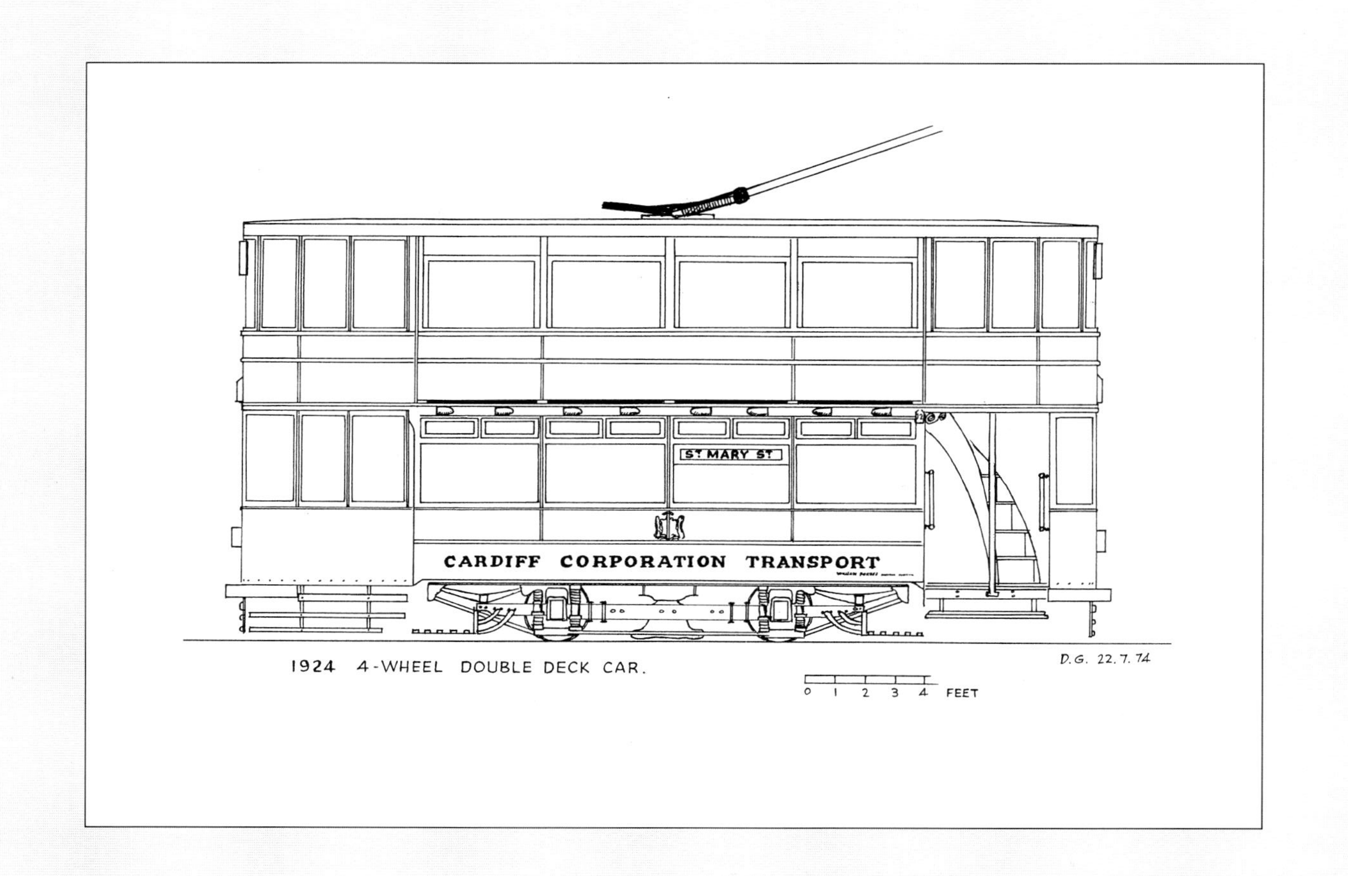

1924 4-WHEEL DOUBLE DECK CAR.

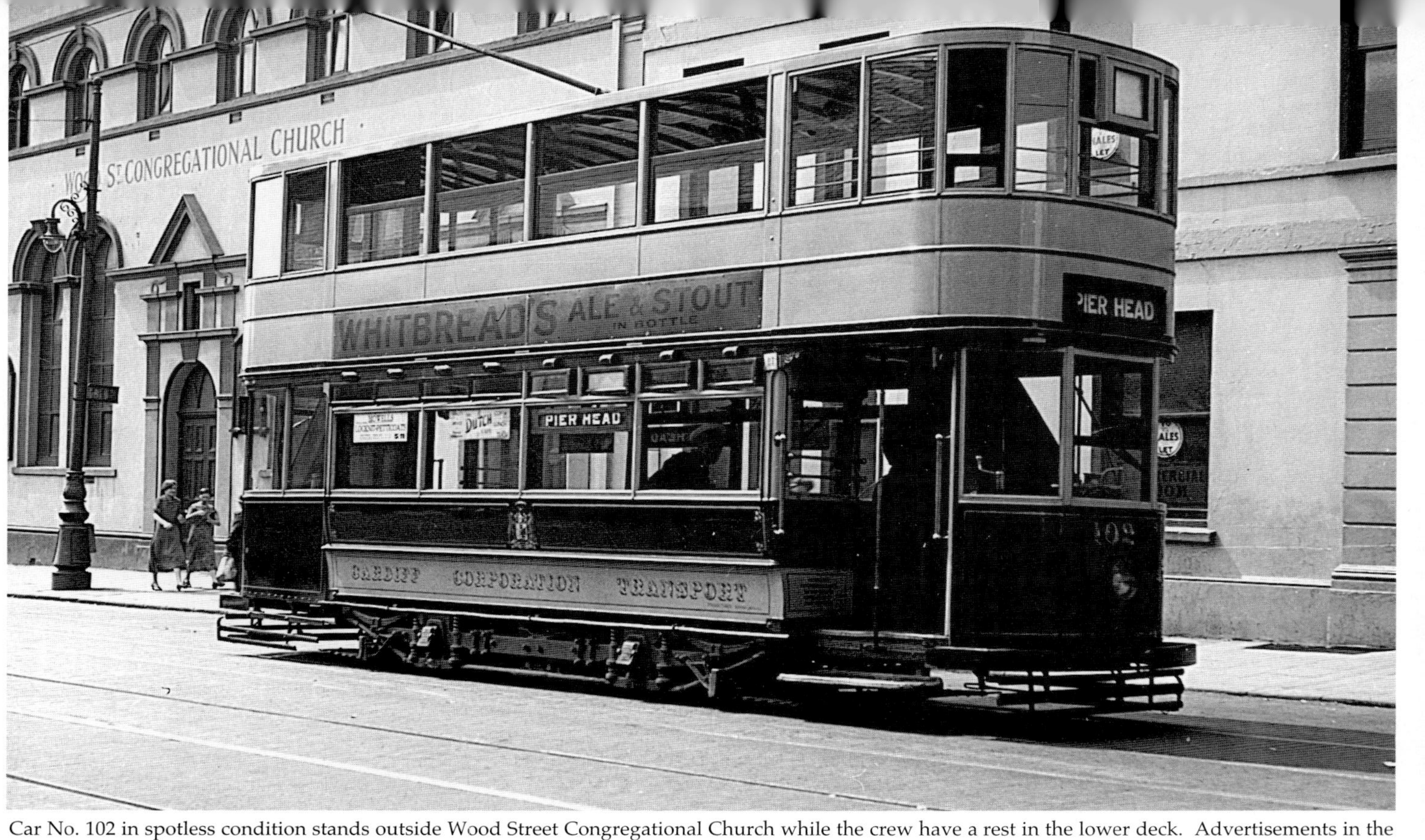

Car No. 102 in spotless condition stands outside Wood Street Congregational Church while the crew have a rest in the lower deck. Advertisements in the windows are for Howells Locknit Petticoats (5/11) and for the Dutch Café (which was in Queen Street). *Author's Collection*

Single-deck car of 1927, built by the Brush Electrical Engineering Co., posed outside Roath depot probably when new. The vehicle has Peckham P.25 maximum-traction trucks and British Thomson-Houston B510E controllers. *Author's Collection*

Four-wheeled car No. 141 (originally 98), kept as a stores vehicle and painted grey. Body by Brush, with original staircase altered to a curved one; Brill 21E truck. Roath depot, 15th April, 1939. *H.B. Priestley*

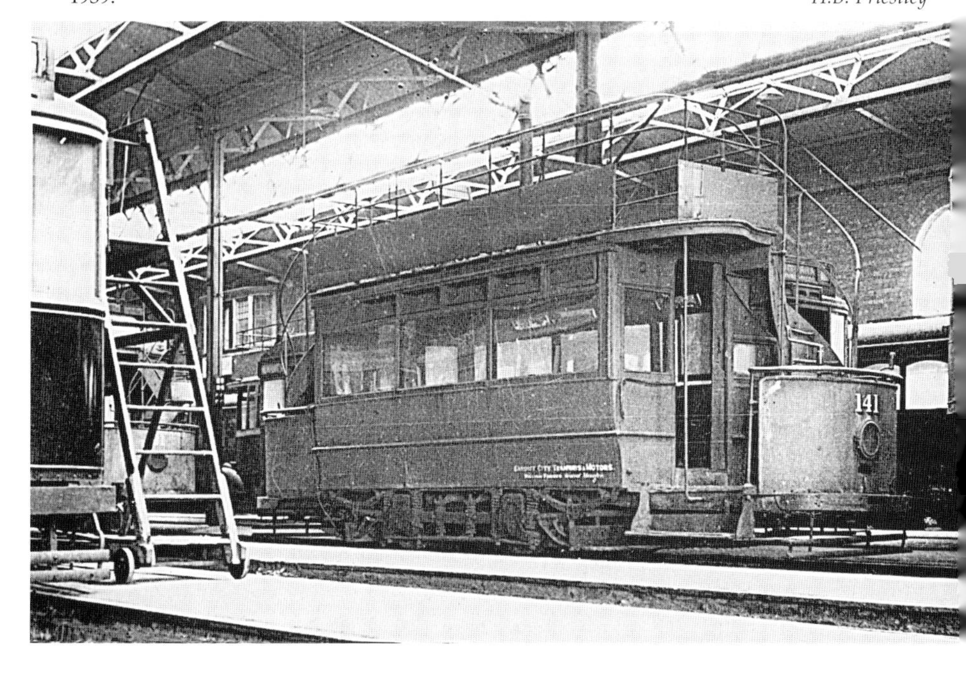

bodies at £1,098 each; BTH for electrical equipment at £510 per equipment; and Peckham for 25 more trucks at £187 each. Delivery was somewhat delayed owing to a strike at Brush; and the final batch of cars (thirty) was ordered, the total cost being £53,850, borrowed from the MoT.

These 55 cars were delivered between February and October 1925; they had B510E controllers and Ackley handbrakes, and they took the numbers 1, 3, 4, 7, 8, 11, 14, 16-19, 21, 25-28, 31, 33, 35-40, 55, 58-60, 63-65, 67-69, 71, 73-75, 77-83, 85-89, 91-94, and 98. There were now 81 top- covered cars, of a standard design, and these would give excellent service for the next 25 years.

After trials with magnetic track brakes and air brakes, the former were found to be better and 75 sets were obtained from BTH in 1926. Another 24 sets arrived later. In 1935 all cars were fitted with Gabriel hand-operated windscreen wipers.

Most of the old cars were disposed of, though some were kept. The first lot to be sold were twenty 4-wheelers to Cashmore's of Newport for £1,000 in April 1924; a year later, 17 more 4-wheelers and 8 bogie double-deck cars were sold for scrap to T.W. Ward of Sheffield. In July 1925, 25 additional old trams were sold to Cashmore's.

The remaining unmodified cars were renumbered 138 (formerly 3, the ticket and parcels car, also used to take money from The Hayes offices to the depot), 139 (formerly 7), 140 (formerly 19), 141 (formerly 98, the last survivor of the slow 95-114 series), 142 (formerly 30), 144 (a 1902 single-decker) and 146 (a 1904 single-decker). These were kept until 1927, most being used on a shuttle service in City Road while Infirmary Junction was being relaid. Afterwards all were scrapped except Nos. 138,140 and 141, which, along with 12, 15 and 61, were kept as stores vehicles, painted grey, the only surviving uncanopied open-top cars.

All the modified cars were retained: the vestibuled bogie open toppers, 4-wheelers, and single-decks (42, 43, 45, 48,115 and 125). The water car No. 131 was painted grey and lost its number.

In July 1925, Mr Horsfield submitted to the Committee drawings, specifications and quotations from Brush for a single-deck car body, with Peckham bogies, and BTH electrical equipment, and recommended that a sample car be bought. Orders were placed, and the car arrived on 3rd March, 1926. It was an extremely fine vehicle, with a domed roof, individual drop-windows, and two saloons, one being for smokers. The 44 seats were transverse, reversible, and were upholstered in basket weave, which certainly was an improvement on the hitherto standard hard wood seats. A teak sliding door gave access to each saloon, with another in the centre of the car.

Body length was 37 ft 6 in. and width 7 ft. Two P25 maximum-traction trucks were fitted, the driving wheels of which were 32¾ in. in diameter and the pony wheels 21¾ in., with a wheelbase of 4 ft 2 in. Two BTH 506A motors of 35/40 hp, B510E controllers, and BTH magnetic track brakes made up the electrical equipment. The number given was 53.

On 12th April, 1926, the City Council approved the expenditure of £73,650 on 30 more new single-deck cars from the same manufacturers, the bodies being £1,503 14s. each, the trucks £350 each, and the electrical equipment, including

track brakes, £647. Delivery was delayed owing to the coal strike; the trams arrived between December 1926 and May 1927 and took the numbers 41, 44, 46, 47, 49-52, 54, 116-124, 126-137. They were put to work on Service 1 (Whitchurch Road via Salisbury Road) and Service 7 (Clive Street and Roath Dock).

Each of these 30 single-deck trams had body pillars and rails of teak, with pitch-pine cantrails. The vestibules were teak-framed, each with a sheet-steel dash on the outside and tongue-and-grooved boards on the inside. Interior mouldings were made of teak and oak, and there were luggage racks on each side above the windows made of aluminium brackets with cord netting. The floor had tongue-and-grooved deal boards ⅞ in. thick with hardwood slats and trapdoors. The arched roof, which had four ventilators, was formed with ash framing and ½ in. tongue-and-grooved pine boards covered with sailcloth.

Glazing was in ¼ in. polished plate ; the side windows, which could slide up and down, were supported on lazytongs and the end windows, except for that in the centre which could be opened, were fixed direct into the framing. Seats, all of woven rattan cane supported by spring frames, were arranged as 32 double transverse with reversible backs and 12 longitudinally at four corners.

The underframe was a combination of rolled-steel sections and teak members, with ¼ in. truss plates secured to each solebar. Trucks were supplied by the Peckham Truck & Engineering Co., with wheel centres by Baker's of Rotherham and 4¼ in.-diameter axles by Hadfield's of Sheffield.

Twenty-three old single-deck cars were sold for scrap to Cashmore's of Newport: ten of the 41-54 series for £350 each, and 13 of the 116-130 batch for £429 each. The numbers of old single decks retained are shown above. Three more old cars were sold in 1930.

Thus, out of a total of 142 tramcars licensed in May 1927, 112 of them were modern; a very satisfactory ratio. 134 trams were licensed each year from 1930 to 1936, and 106 in 1937, 1938 and 1939.

It is of interest that Cardiff's lowbridge cars, the first of their kind, excited considerable attention from other tramway operators, and deputations from Swansea, Edinburgh, the London County Council and elsewhere came to Cardiff to inspect them. Swansea indeed bought 13 lowbridge cars from Brush to a very similar design to Cardiff's.

The proportions of this type were excellent; it was not so tall and top-heavy in appearance as the normal design, and was not so high off the ground, a feature that was most noticeable when one could be seen standing alongside an older vestibuled open-topper.

It is one of the tragedies of British tramways that no sooner had their owners acquired new cars than they decided to scrap the system, so that the new trams always had a very short life compared to that of the cars they were supposed to have replaced. This was the case in Cardiff; the superb new single-deck cars, once described as the best trams Cardiff ever had, were on the Salisbury Road line only a short while before its closure; then, when Service 7 closed in 1936, there was no more work for them.

On 31st October, 1936, William Forbes published a document giving a detailed description of these cars and offering them for disposal; it records that they were in excellent running condition, each having run on average only

about 100,000 miles. Apparently there were no takers and so all 31 single-deckers were stored. Forbes issued the document again, on 30th August, 1939, at the same time adding four of the old rebuilt single-deckers and six open-top cars to the list of cars for disposal. In January 1940 the Brush-built single-deck cars were at last sold for £52 10*s*. each. Eighteen of them were purchased by the Para Electric Railways of Belem, Brazil; they were removed for shipment from Roath Depot on 1st April, 1940. They ran in Para until 1947.

There were still seven or eight open-top cars in service up to the early part of 1946, in regular peak-hour use between Newport Road and Victoria Park; but they were all withdrawn shortly afterwards and run to Clare Road depot for breaking up. Nos. 22 and 84 were the last two observed in use, on 27th and 25th March, 1946, respectively. Of the top-covered cars, all were still in service except No. 78, which had been withdrawn for spares before 1940. Following accident damage, Nos. 7, 21, 62, 89 and 98 were broken up early in 1947, and many more followed as routes were withdrawn. From August 1949 onwards trams were broken up and burned by a contractor at the rear of Roath depot, and by November only 29 cars remained active.

Six cars, including No. 2, had their trolley poles fitted with collector skates of trolley bus type, replacing their trolley wheels, shortly before closure. Inside the dash panel was a notice informing the driver that the car had been so fitted.

All the electric cars, with the exception of water car No. 131, were scrapped. Surprisingly, however, a Cardiff horse tram has been saved. Discovered by two 17-year-olds in 1968, Max Hampson and John Winter, the car had been in use as a tea stall in Roath Dock from about 1907 until 1966 and was about to be broken up. The car was removed to S. Andrews' Garage in City Road. In 1971 the new owners donated the car to the National Museum of Wales, and when the Welsh Industrial and Maritime Museum, Bute Street, Cardiff, was opened in 1977 the car went there. In 1980 work started on its restoration, which was completed in June 1983. The car, numbered 21, was found to have been used on the Cathays-St John's Square route (opened in December 1886) and so has been painted yellow - the Cathays route colour. On 24th September, 1986, No. 21 took part in the Roath depot closing ceremony when, hauled by a borrowed pair of horses, it gave rides to invited guests.

Water-tank car used for rail-cleaning, built in 1902 and inside Roath depot in the 1930s.
Author's Collection

Roath Park terminus, and the water car, with driver Gerry Wakeling on the platform, is about to be passed by car No. 70 as it approaches the waiting city-bound passengers on 1st May, 1949.
Ian L. Wright

Chapter Fourteen

Water Car No. 131

On 11th February, 1902, a 1,000 gallon rail-cleaning car was ordered from Dick, Kerr & Co. Ltd at a price of £600; and later that year the complete car was delivered from the Electric Railway & Tramway Carriage Works Ltd. It had a Brill 21E truck, 25 hp DK 25A motors and DK DB1 Form B controllers; it was completely open, with a centrally-mounted water tank and at each end a broom with water-spray behind. No number was carried until 1905, when it became No. 131. Livery was dark red overall. For many years modern historians had believed that the car had been built in 1905 by Brush, but recent researches by J.H. Price have confirmed that ER&TCW were the builders, in 1902. Around 1908/9 (and certainly by 1913) the tank was enclosed in a body of unusual design, with timber planking and rounded mouldings similar to those on railway carriages. This body was painted lake and cream, lettered CARDIFF CITY TRAMWAYS (the first two words forming an arc over the third), and the numerals were standard gold transfers shaded with blue. The platforms were canopied, and partly glazed at the sides.

From about 1916 onwards until 1950 its livery was grey, unlined. The number 131 was carried on the side panel until about 1926, after which no number was displayed. Unofficially the car was named 'Polly'. Officially the car did not exist, for it was never shown in 'returns'.

The car was transferred to stores and general permanent way work in 1920, and was equipped for rail-grinding. Before this, it used to go out on night work towing two grinding machines behind it. Also recalled is that No. 131 was often used to take the traffic superintendent H. David, home to Cathays after the passenger cars had returned to the depot for the night.

In 1919 No. 131 had been fitted with a slipper brake. H.B. Priestley, who knew the car from 1913 onwards, believed that the brooms and sprinklers resulted from a convenient arrangement with the Highways Department rather than from any external obligation.

In 1947 the original motors were replaced, owing to armature trouble, by a pair of GEC type GE200K motors taken from one of the withdrawn bogie open-top cars. The car was still in use on rail-grinding duties right up to 1949, its regular driver being Gerry Wakeling. One could see No. 131 on a Sunday morning, perhaps at Roath Park terminus, or by the Talygarn Street crossover.

From late 1949 local tramway enthusiast Ian L. Wright corresponded with John H. Price, of the Light Railway Transport League's Museum Committee, on the subject of the water car's preservation, which was initiated by Mr Price. It was clear that if anything was to be saved it would have to be through the efforts of amateurs; the Transport Committee had no intention of preserving the car or any of the passenger fleet. Mr Wright's view was that the General Manager was unco-operative and it would have been useless to make the suggestion to him. Nevertheless, the LRTL's Museum Committee chairman, Robert B. Parr, would write to Cardiff Corporation to secure the preservation of

a standard car by the Corporation, as well as the water car because of its unusual interest.

Early in 1950 the General Manager, J.F. Siddall, informed J.H. Price that the Transport Committee at its meeting of 19th January had approved the idea of preserving the water car, partly because it was 'not included in the schedule of tramcars for disposal'. (Because officially it did not exist, it had been overlooked!) The decision of the Transport Committee was confirmed by the City Council at its meeting of 6th February, 1950, and the car was presented to the LRTL Museum Committee free of charge.

Now the problem of where to keep it emerged. Felix Cunuder, the Transport Department's engineer and rolling stock superintendent, promised to do all he could to house it inside Roath Depot, and in fact it remained there until March 1951. Ian Wright and his fellow enthusiasts wished to carry out restoration work and repaint the car, the cost of this falling upon these men. The Transport Department took no interest whatever, although it agreed to supply the necessary paint at a cost of £3 17*s*. 10*d*.

During 1950 the volunteers - Ian Wright, Robert Jones, Derek Chaplin, Geoffrey Booth and Ted Collins - worked on the car in Roath Depot. The lower portion of the dash, which was corroded by salt, was replaced by new aluminium sheet; a new lifeguard (purchased from Leeds for £1) was fixed; the car was repainted in crimson lake and cream and transfers were applied. The car now (it was hoped) looked as it did around 1913.

Although No. 131 was very small, it took up more space than the Transport Department cared to give up and so, in December 1950, Mr Siddall informed Ian Wright that as the space was required for 'other purposes' the car would have to go. So, on 29th March, 1951, it was removed from the depot to Flottmann Drill Works, Allensbank Road, by Robert Wynn & Sons, and Ian's pocket was lighter by £12 10*s*. He then had to purchase tarpaulin sheets to protect the car, and they cost a further £9.

This too was only a temporary home, and on 27th October, 1952, No. 131 left Cardiff altogether - and to date it has never returned. The second move was to Price, Walker's timber yard, Gloucester, where at least the car could be housed in a shed. Robert Wynn & Sons' bill for the removal was £30, of which two-thirds was paid by Ian Wright and one-third by John Price.

In 1955 the LRTL Museum Committee was superseded by a new Tramway Museum Society, which became the owners of No. 131. After much hunting a permanent site for a tramway museum was found at Crich, Derbyshire, in 1959; and it was Cardiff 131 that had the honour of being the first of many cars to arrive there, on 8th May, 1959. After spending some years there, first under tarpaulins in the open air, then immured in one of the sheds, it was moved to the Museum's store at Clay Cross on 14th May 1971, where it was not on view to the public. As far as is known, no work has ever been done to it since the 1950 restoration, nor has it ever been made to run under power. Its controllers were transferred to another car, Leicester Corporation No. 76, when that was restored to working order.

According to J.H. Price the Tramway Museum Society offered No. 131 to the Welsh Industrial and Maritime Museum on indefinite loan but was not

prepared to *donate* the car because of a clause in the TMS Constitution requiring a two-thirds majority vote of members present at an annual general meeting. Unfortunately, although the Welsh Industrial and Maritime Museum would have preferred outright ownership of the car, it would not have been able to accept it because of the lack of covered accommodation. To the TMS the main value of No. 131 seems to be its Brill 21E truck, which could be used at some future date to keep a working car running, the defective truck then being transferred to the water car, or even (according to Mr Price) having its original truck replaced by a wooden replica.

Two other reasons for the TMS not wishing to relinquish ownership of No. 131 were that it might be required as an illuminated car, and that the number of countries represented in the fleet at Crich would be reduced - this being the only car from Wales.

Cardiff water car No. 131 was acquired for preservation and repainted attractively by enthusiasts. For a short time the Transport Department allowed it to be kept inside Roath depot but in March 1951 it had to be removed. No. 131 is here shown on 10th January, 1951, before the removal. *Ian L. Wright*

Reconditioned bogie double-deck car of 1902, showing Brill 22E maximum-traction truck, inside Roath Depot, 7th September, 1937. *H.B. Priestley*

Reconditioned bogie open-top car No. 30, still in superb condition after 35 years. The small lettering on the bulkhead reads: 'Wait until the car stops.' Roath depot, 1st January, 1938. *H.B. Priestley*

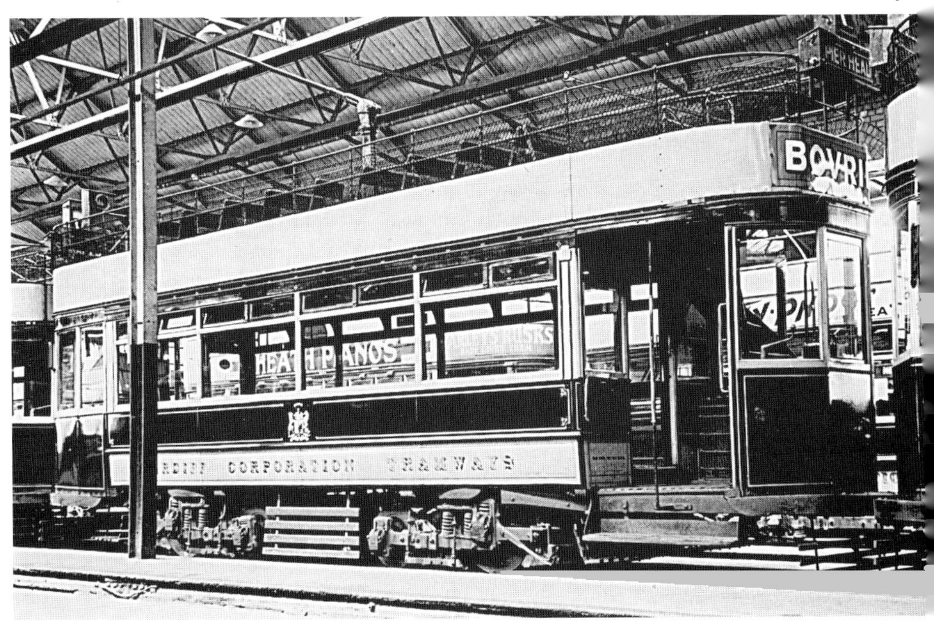

Chapter Fifteen

Tramcar Livery

Livery throughout the life of the Cardiff tramways was cream upper works and rocker panel, and crimson lake for the dashes and waist panel, all lined out in gold. The words CARDIFF CORPORATION TRAMWAYS appeared in large gold letters on the rocker panel, and the city coat of arms in the centre of the waist panel. From 1934, TRANSPORT was substituted for TRAMWAYS on repainting. Inscribed on the lower panel of each bulkhead, on the passenger's left as he boarded, was PASSENGERS/ENTERING OR LEAVING/THE CAR WHILST IN/MOTION DO SO AT/THEIR OWN RISK. The fleet number, carried on the dash above the headlamp, was displayed in gold numeral transfers, blocked blue and shaded black, six inches high.

The standard of coach-painting was extremely high and, as photographs of the trams show, the result was a fleet of smart and dignified vehicles. The painting specification has come to hand; this applies to cars in the 1930s:

First coat - white lead.
Second coat - cream body colour, using paint by Williamson's of Ripon.
Third coat - gloss cream (Williamson's paint).
Fourth coat - hard body varnish. This was then flatted, transfers were added, and a finishing varnish (Williamson's) applied.

For the crimson lake areas, the following specification was used:

Undercoat - Tuscan Red.
Second coat - Crimson lake colour coat, made by Williamson's.
Third coat - gloss crimson lake. This was translucent, and allowed the reflection of the colour coat to show through, resulting in a colour subtlety that is impossible to simulate today, as these paints are no longer made.

Finally, high-grade pale quality varnishes were applied.

The lining on the waist panel consisted of an outer line ⅝ in. wide and an inner line ¼ in. wide, with a floral design at each corner. The car roof was grey, and the underframe red bitumastic paint. When the wartime grey came in, this consisted merely of two coats, an undercoat and a gloss finish; cars known to have been painted this colour were Nos. 14, 28, 36, 38, 40, 80, 82, 85, 87, 91, 109 and 114, from 1943 until 1946. Few cars were repainted during their last years. No. 11 received a repaint in lake and cream in 1946 and in January 1947 No. 88 was repainted in the old livery. In the final days of the trams, the red and cream were only just visible under a layer of dirt - an agonising contrast to the spotless condition in which they were kept in pre-war days.

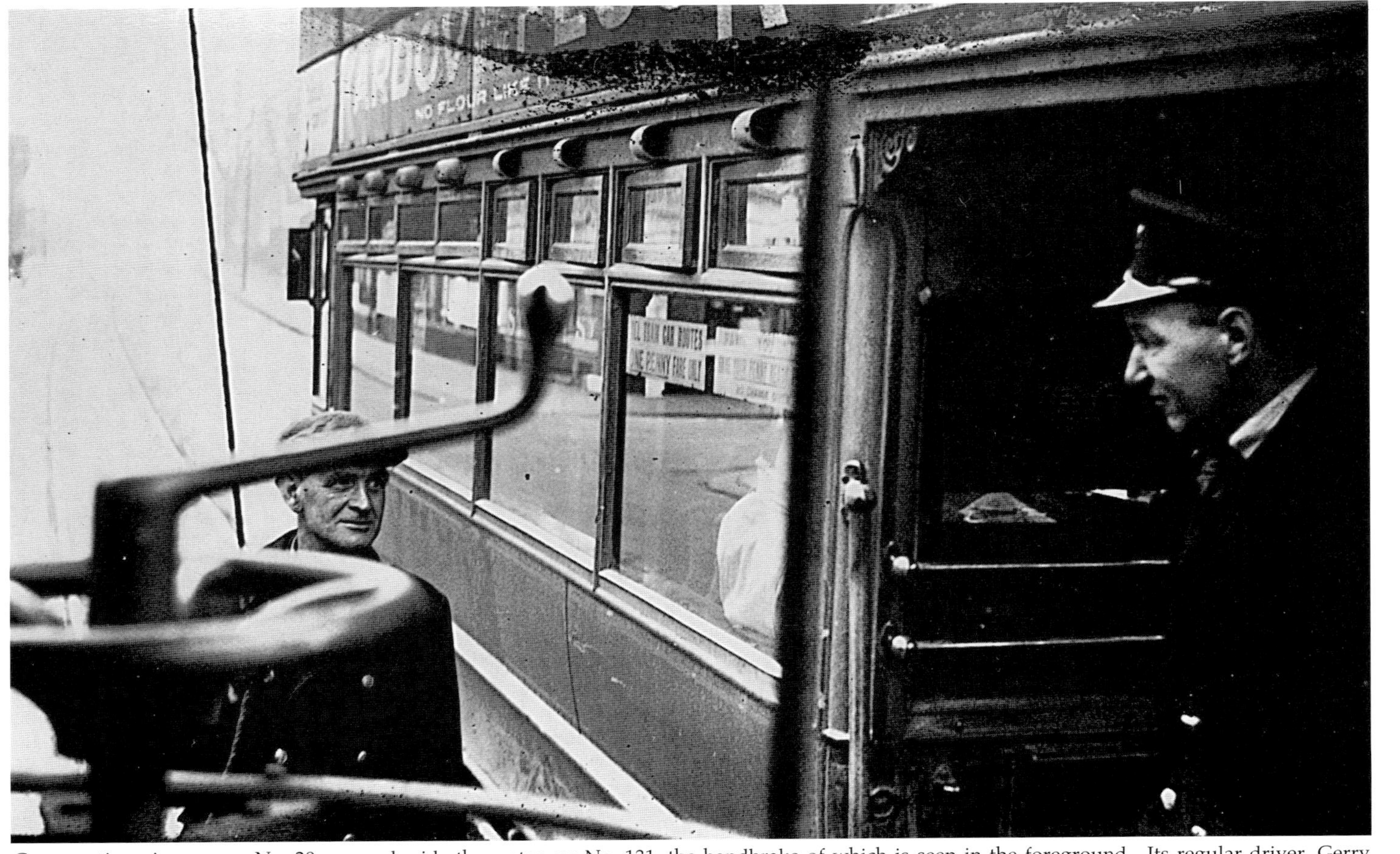

Conversation-piece as car No. 20 pauses beside the water car No. 131, the handbrake of which is seen in the foreground. Its regular driver, Gerry Wakeling, is holding the trolley rope. Whitchurch Road, 20th February, 1949.

Chapter Sixteen

Tramwaymen and Working Conditions

Takeover of the Tramways Company by the Corporation must have been welcomed by the tramwaymen, for their working hours were reduced from 65 a week of five days (since 1896) to 54 a week of six days, with no reduction of pay, which was 6½*d*. per hour for motormen, and 5¾*d*. per hour for conductors. Up to 1896, work had been from 8 am to 11 pm with a 1¼ hour lunch break. Under the Corporation, men were paid time-and-a-half for Sunday work and double pay for Bank Holiday work. The men had a Sick Benefit Society, and they also received from the Corporation sick pay at the rate of 50 per cent of whatever sum they might receive from that sick benefit.

Rules for tramwaymen seem today to be very strict, and transport undertakings of today, with their perennial staff shortages, must sigh for the days when they could dismiss a man for the most trivial offence, and there would always be someone waiting to take his place. Smartness was considered to be of great importance. Extracts from the 1905 rule-book indicate that:

> The uniform clothing must be kept neat and clean, the cloth brushed daily and kept in good order. All buttons, numbers and badges must be kept bright and polished. The tunic and overcoat must be worn close-buttoned, the cap worn without decoration of any kind.
>
> *And again*: Drivers and Conductors must report at the Depot Office neat and clean in appearance. They must present themselves 15 minutes before the appointed time for their car to start, and examine the car to see that it is in order and properly cleaned and fit for service.

Conductors were not expected to slouch all over the car, but to stand upright on the rear platform when not collecting fares, facing the street, and giving assistance to passengers. 'Suspension will follow in every reported case of fares being collected as passengers are leaving the car.' Imagine!

However, they were not required to accept sovereigns from passengers; they were authorised to ask such passengers to go and get change, or take the passenger's name and address if he refused.

Some men had not received their uniforms by September 1902. The uniform itself was blue serge with brass buttons and high button-up collar which had the man's number on it. The city coat of arms was embossed on the buttons. Round the cuffs and running from top to bottom of the trousers was a ¼ in. wide red piping; the epaulettes had a rim of red piping. This outfit was worn winter and summer, with a heavy serge overcoat in winter. The only concession to summer was that between 1st May and 30th September every year drivers fitted a piece of shiny white material over their cap tops, presumably to reflect the glare of the sun.

Most of the men were members of the Amalgamated Association of Tramway and Vehicle Workers, later the Transport & General Workers Union. Non-unionism was rather frowned on by the Corporation, but they could not compel

men to join. A few strikes were recorded over the years: one in 1912, where the Lord Mayor was disappointed that no recognition was given to the workers who had loyally 'stuck by the city'; and of course the General Strike, previously described. There was an unofficial strike from the 6th to the 17th March, 1948, and all services were suspended; the main beneficiary was British Railways, as all the local trains ran packed to capacity during this strike.

From 1902, lads were employed as pointsmen at 10s. a week, working from 8 am to 11 pm, five days a week. A pointsman/signalman was retained at Infirmary Junction until 1936, when he was replaced by an automatic point turner.

Apparently tramwaymen in the 1900s were in the habit of soliciting subscriptions from passengers every Christmas. This practice, a hangover from Company days, was roundly condemned by the Corporation.

In 1907, to reduce the wages bill, the management dismissed 23 cleaners and replaced them with boys; even inspectors were down to the absolute minimum. Total saving was over £3,000 a year

From 1908, men were paid double time for any overtime worked after 12.30 am, but cars seldom worked to such a late hour. At that time there were 18 spare drivers and 36 spare conductors to cover sickness; the Chairman thought it very necessary to keep such a large number. The manager considered that 'Cardiff is still looked upon as a town where tramway employees are particularly favourably situated, and is held up by employees in these towns as an example of labour conditions as nearly as possible perfect.' Indeed, when Christmas fell on a Sunday, in one year, the platform staff were paid double time for both that day and Boxing Day.

In 1919 the working hours were reduced from 54 to 48 per week, which meant that more men were needed, and a further reduction was made in 1928 to 42 hours a week, with the hours worked on split duties to be no more than 33⅓ per cent of the total. At various times the union had made attempts to get 'spreadover' turns abolished, but naturally without success, as the necessity of having more cars on the road during the busy periods than the slack time meant that some men would have to work on both 'peaks', with rest during the middle of the day. The maximum time on a 'spreadover' was about 10½ hours. Drivers were now paid £3 a week; in 1926 there were 315 of these, and 338 conductors.

Tramwaymen had their own nicknames for various features of the system, such as the 'Siberian Route' for No. 7, possibly owing to the barren appearance of the Splott area; and Infirmary Junction was jocularly known as 'Faith, Hope and Charity', because of the presence there of a church, a hospital and a bank.

Henry North was one of several long-serving tramway employees, having started as a trace-horse boy in 1901 and graduating to chief inspector. From 1902 he was a points-boy, but soon became a conductor. Then in succession he was depot supervisor, ticket-checking inspector, accident inquiry inspector, district inspector and finally chief inspector. Interviewed by the *South Wales Echo* shortly before his retirement in February 1952 he recalled :

> The new-fangled electric trams caused quite a disturbance. People used to stand in the streets and just watch them. Crowds of people came down from the valleys to see them.

With the Corporation in charge of the tramways discipline became very strict, and to be called before the traffic supervisor usually meant dismissal or at least temporary suspension. But there was a family feeling about the whole business. There were regular conductors and drivers on the same route all the time and there were also regular passengers. It was all very friendly. Often we would delay the tram for one of the regulars who happened to be a bit late.

I got my conductor's licence at the age of 16½, and it was no easy thing to get in those days. You had to appear before a committee at the Town Hall and were given a test on street names, among other things.

The secret of success in the transport department is readiness at all times to serve the public. I was a public servant and proud of it.

Another employee with 50 years' service was interviewed by the *South Wales Echo* in May 1978. Ivor Brown started as tramway parcels messenger boy in 1928, working from the parcels office in The Hayes. The office later became the Hayes Island Snack Bar. He recalled :

For fourpence a team of eight messengers would deliver parcels from the big shops to any part of the city served by the trams. We wore a smart uniform and had a reputation of being able to deliver a parcel within an hour of it being deposited at the depot. In the 1930s I became a conductor and was later promoted to inspector. There was something romantic about the trams.

At the time of his retirement in 1978 Mr Brown was assistant traffic superintendent.

Chapter Seventeen

Tramway Services

This subject, so far as Cardiff is concerned, is a complex one, since the city has had a tradition of altering routes every few years, presumably because the authorities felt that by running a car to 'B' instead of 'A' they might perhaps increase revenue.

The building up of routes from the opening has been described; by the end of 1904 there were now so many services that severe congestion and 'bunching' were commonplace. Apparently the Tramways Committee had up to now acceded to any request from the public to introduce new services, but it was time to call a halt. Complaints had been received that often three cars would be standing at Canton terminus and blocking the road. With three services to Canton, each running frequently, it was hardly surprising; the situation being aggravated by the single track sections between Radnor Road and Beda Road, and Bute Street Bridge to Canal Bridge, where a car waiting to enter the single line would be caught up by the car behind it. Of the three Canton services, the Pier Head and Roath Park ones were remunerative, but the Wood Street via Neville Street one was not; it required only two cars anyway. Mr Ellis, in drawing up his plans for improved services, deplored the great number of cross-town routes, considering it ridiculous that passengers should be dragged from Queen Street to Castle Street via The Hayes and St Mary Street when, by getting off at Queen Street and walking a few yards along Duke Street, they could continue their journey two or three cars ahead of the one they had just alighted from! So he eliminated the Roath Park to Canton service, at the same time extending the Pier Head-Penylan Road service to Roath Park terminus, with an 8 min. frequency. The Penylan Road cars now ran to The Hayes (Royal Arcade) only, with an 8 min. service, giving Albany Road a tram every 4 min. Canton now had only one service - that to Pier Head, running every 4 min., the Neville Street service being withdrawn. After 7.30 pm, there was a 5 min. service from Canton to Monument, with alternate trams extended to Pier Head.

Other service alterations made at the same time were to the Broadway cars, now to run to Pier Head until 7.30 pm, then terminate at Mill Lane, with a 6 min. service; Aberdovey Street to The Hayes (Royal Arcade) via Glossop Road, every 15 min.; and Splott to Grangetown via Custom House Street, every 9 min. Cathedral Road to Clarence Road was every 5 min. to 7.30 pm, then every 6 min.

Turning his attention to the recently-opened Whitchurch Road line, Ellis considered that the amount of traffic did not justify running every car from St Mary Street through to Talygarn Street terminus; so there was now to be a 4 min. service to Woodville Road/Crwys Road with alternate cars extended to Talygarn Street. Finally, there would be two special cars working in the morning, midday and evening busy periods on each of the following services; Canton to Clarence Road direct, Cathedral Road to Clarence Road direct, and Broadway to the Monument.

These revised services now required a total of 77 cars (71 less specials), as

opposed to 86 previously, and after 7.30 pm, only 58. This does not include workmen's cars, of which there were 23 in service, and this traffic was not disturbed by the alterations. These cars ran out early, the first leaving the depot before 5 am. The traffic finished at about 8 am, but the cars were kept on for the heavy rushes between 8.30 and 9.30, after which they returned to the depot. They returned to traffic shortly after 4 pm, but again after the workmen's traffic had ceased the cars kept in circulation for business people between 5.30 and 6.30 pm. The running of workmen's cars was highly uneconomic, and the Corporation intensely disliked having to do it, but was compelled to by the Act. In 1907, the Manager was authorised to discontinue the Broadway-Victoria Park and Broadway-Pier Head cars, if he wished. Shortly after he had been granted absolute control of the managing of the tramways, he did in fact withdraw the Cathedral Road-Docks workmen's car, in May 1907, and in his report he stated:

> This has been withdrawn for the simple reason that it has not been patronised except by a very limited number of workmen; and . . . the receipts from these cars only average a little over 4*d*. per car mile, and if the responsibility for improving the results of the tramways during the next year is to be thrown on to me, I do not think I am justified in continuing to run any unremunerative cars anywhere.
>
> The tramways in the past have been very seriously handicapped by the number of cars which have been run solely for the convenience of the working men, at ridiculously low fare, and if the tramways in the future are to show a surplus, they cannot bear these burdens any longer.

The legality of this move was questioned; the Corporation was legally obliged to run two workmen's cars each way on every weekday, under Section 34 of the 1898 Act which stated:

> The Corporation at all times after the opening of the tramways for public traffic shall and they are hereby required to run at least two carriages each way every morning in the week and every evening in the week (Sundays, Christmas Day and Good Friday excepted) not later than seven in the morning or earlier than five in the evening.

This was taken to mean two cars on *each individual route,* so demands were made for the reinstatement of the Cathedral Road car. But Ellis stood by his action, maintaining that it was necessary only to provide two cars each way or four cars *in total,* and many more than that were in fact provided, so he reckoned that the Tramways Committee were not doing too badly! He added,

> I am very much in sympathy with the working classes, and more so with clerks and young girls who earn a low rate of wage, and yet have to keep up a certain amount of appearance, and would do anything to assist them, but a Tramways system is a commercial undertaking and must be worked as such, and not as a Benevolent Institution.

So the car was not restored; it had in fact been placed on the Canton route with an increase in revenue being the result.

In 1913, a system of service numbers was introduced and the route-indicating discs and lights abolished. Up till 1920, the routes were as follows:

1	Whitchurch Road and St Mary Street via Salisbury Road.
1	Whitchurch Road and St Mary Street via City Road (Peak hours)
2	Newport Road (Broadway) and Pier Head.
3	Penylan Road and Pier Head.
4	Roath Park and St Mary Street.
5	Victoria Park and Pier Head via High Street.
6	Cathedral Road and Clarence Road via High Street.
7	Carlisle Street and Grangetown via Bute Terrace (Off-peak).
7	Roath Dock, Splott and Grangetown via Bute Terrace (Peak hours).
8	The Hayes and Roath Dock, Splott via Glossop Road.
9	Roath Park and Victoria Park via High Street (Sundays only).
EX	Victoria Park and Clarence Road via Neville Street (Peak hours).
EX	Cathedral Road and Clarence Road via Lower Cathedral Road (Peak hours).
EX	Whitchurch Road and Roath Dock, Splott via Glossop Road (Peak hours).
-	Pier Head and Whitchurch Road via City Road (Peak hours).
EX	Victoria Park and St Mary Street (Peak hours).

In 1920 a 1A (St Mary Street and Crwys Road via Salisbury Road), 1B (Whitchurch Road, City Road and Market Road, Canton) and a 5A (Mill Lane, Castle Street and Victoria Park) were introduced. Later the No. 3 was extended to Roath Park and the 4 altered to run between Penylan Road and Market Road. However, cross-city trams would not be crawling round Working Street and High Street for very much longer, for the opening in June 1924 of Duke Street for trams caused further service alterations. Nos. 1, 2, 5, 6 and 7 remained as before. New services are detailed below:

1A	Whitchurch Road and Cathedral Road via Duke Street.
1B	Whitchurch Road and St Mary Street via City Road (Peak hours).
2A	Newport Road and Victoria Park via Duke Street.
3	Roath Park and Pier Head.
4	Roath Park and Market Road via Duke Street.
4A	Penylan Road and St Mary Street (Peak hours).
5A	Victoria Park and St Mary Street (Peak hours).
6A	Clarence Road and Wood Street (Peak hours).
7	Splott and Grangetown via Bute Terrace.
8	Splott and Victoria Park via Glossop Road and Duke Street.
9	Roath Park and Victoria Park via Duke Street (Sundays).
10	Roath Park and St Mary Street via The Hayes (Sundays).
11	Whitchurch Road and Pier Head via City Road (Peak hours).
12	Splott and The Hayes via Glossop Road.
13	Cathedral Road and Clarence Road via Clare Street (Peak hours).
14	Victoria Park and Clarence Road via Neville Street (Peak hours).
15	Mackintosh Place and St Mary Street (Peak hours).
16	Whitchurch Road and Clarence Road via City Road, Duke Street and Clare Road.
-	Whitchurch Road and Splott (Peak hours).

Services terminating at St Mary Street travelled inwards via The Hayes and outwards via High Street, except the 10, which operated via The Hayes both ways. Service 12, renumbered from service 8 in June 1924, suffered many alterations. In 1927 it was extended from The Hayes to St Mary Street; then on 16th December, 1930, it became Splott, Queen Street, High Street, Wood Street

and Clive Street Grange; because of poor receipts it was curtailed to run between Carlisle Street and Clive Street from 11th January, 1932. It was then found that the service between Penarth Road Junction and Clive Street terminus was not justified during evenings, so it was further curtailed to run from Clive Street Library. Finally, late in 1934, it was diverted to Clarence Road, with a 12 minute service, giving a combined interval of 6 minutes from Wood Street to Clarence Road, with the No. 6 service. The 12 was withdrawn two years later.

On 9th July, 1925, an experimental service, Clarence Road to Roath Park, started, but it is not recorded what happened to it. It could not have lasted very long.

By 1928 service 4 had become Roath Park-St Mary Street, and services 1B, 11 and 15 had been withdrawn. After the closure of the Salisbury Road service in January 1930, tram route 1A (Whitchurch Road and Cathedral Road) became No. 1. In 1931 all-day short-workings of routes 2 and 5, running to St Mary Street, were brought in (2B and 5A respectively). An all-day service 4A ran between Penylan Road and St Mary Street. Services 10 and 13 ceased and the 16 ran only on Saturdays from noon. More all-day short-workings were later brought in: 6A (Clarence Road-Wood Street); 7A (Grangetown and Monument via Penarth Road); and 8A (Victoria Park and Infirmary). These were designed to augment the basic service at busy times; for example, the 7A, introduced in December 1934, ran every 12-13 minutes, providing a 6-7 min. interval with the 7, at the following times: Saturdays Excepted, 8 am to 9.15 am, 12 noon to 2.30 pm, 4.45 to 7.10 pm; Saturdays Only, 8 am to 9.15 am, and 12 noon to approximately 10.45 pm.

Tram services as at 1930/1 were as follows:

1	Whitchurch Road, City Road, Duke Street and Cathedral Road, every 7-9 min.
2	Newport Road and Pier Head, every 5-8 min.
2A	Newport Road and Victoria Park, every 12 min.
3	Roath Park and Pier Head, every 7-9 min.
4	Roath Park and St Mary Street, every 7-9 min.
4A	Penylan Road and Town.
5	Victoria Park, St Mary Street and Pier Head, every 5-7 min.
6	Cathedral Road, St Mary Street and Clarence Road, every 7-9 min.
7	Roath Dock, Splott, the Monument and Clive Street, Grangetown, every 12 min.
8	Roath Dock, Splott, Queen Street and Victoria Park.
9	Roath Park and Victoria Park, every 12 min.
12	Roath Dock, Queen Street, Wood Street, and Clive Street, every 12 min.
14	Victoria Park, Neville Street and Clarence Road.
16	Whitchurch Road and Clarence Road (Saturdays only).

Note that service 9 had become daily, but this was short-lived as it was withdrawn on 23rd April, 1934, for the same reasons as those given in 1904: namely, that cars on this service clashed with others to Victoria Park at places such as City Road Junction and High Street. It was pointed out that there was a 3 minute service between the city centre and Victoria Park; also a 3 minute service between the city centre and Roath Park, with a 'spot' connection; and a transfer system was operated for the convenience of passengers between

Victoria Park and Roath Park. Moreover, on Bank Holidays, and when there were fetes at Roath Park, the direct service continued to run.

Following the closure of Grangetown-Splott line, service 8 was arranged to run between Victoria Park and Adamsdown Square, but was abandoned in February 1940. Services 7 and 12 were replaced by motor buses.

Over the years, the number of services had varied from just a few to rather too many, and once again the time had come to reduce the amount. From 28th April 1940, the routes were as follows:

1 Whitchurch Road and St Mary Street (inward via The Hayes, outward via High Street).
2 Newport Road and Pier Head (via High Street; peak services from Newport Road worked inward via The Hayes).
2A, 5 and 6 - As before.
3 Roath Park and Pier Head (Peak only, southwards via The Hayes, northwards via High Street).
4 Roath Park and St Mary Street (Off peak only, via Duke Street).
8 Cathedral Road and Newport Road.
16 Clarence Road and Newport Road.

Then, in mid-1941, re-laying of Wood Street Junction with the north curve taken out prevented Service 6 from working throughout; it was split into two sections, becoming 6 - Cathedral Road and St Mary Street, and 6A - Wood Street and Clarence Road. Transfer fares were in operation. At Wood Street, trams terminated at a hitherto little-used siding; at Clarence Road they had to stop slightly short of the old terminus, because the newly-erected trolley bus wiring, the positive wire of which was used by the trams, turned off into Hunter Street to form a terminal loop for the future trolley buses, and naturally no track was laid. Trolley buses took over on route 6 on 1st March, 1942, with P.A.Y.E., and in May of that year a further reorganisation of tramway services was carried out, in connection with a flat fare of 1d. (P.A.Y.E. not being installed on the tram routes until 1943). The 1*d*. fare gave a maximum ride of 4 miles before 8 am and three miles after that time.

Services were now as follows:

Until 8 am (Weekdays)

1 Whitchurch Road and Pier Head.
2 Newport Road and Pier Head.
3 Roath Park and Pier Head.
5 Victoria Park and Pier Head via St Mary Street
6 Cathedral Road and St Mary Street
8 Victoria Park and Newport Road via Queen Street
14 Victoria Park and Clare Road Depot.

After 8 am

1A/1B Whitchurch Road and St Mary Street.
2A/2B Newport Road and St Mary Street.
4A/4B Roath Park and St Mary Street.
(The 'A' routes travelled inward via The Hayes and outward via Duke Street; the 'B' routes inward via Duke Street and outward via The Hayes).

5A	Victoria Park and Bute Street Junction via St Mary Street.
6	Cathedral Road and St Mary Street.
8	Victoria Park and Windsor Place ('Capitol').
16	The Hayes (Royal Arcade) and Pier Head.

These services were retained until their closure; when the 16 was withdrawn in 1946, Bute Street also lost all the early morning services of the other routes.

Timetables

1902 Timetables

The following are the timetables in operation on all electric tram services during September 1902.

Canton and Roath Park Route

Clive Road to Town Centre:
7.45, 7.52, 8.00 am and every 7½ min. till 10.45 pm; 10.52 and 11.00 pm to Penylan Road ; and 11.07 till 11.37 pm to Town Centre only.
Town Centre to Roath Park:
8.03, 8.10, 8.18 am and every 7½ min. till 11.03 pm then 11.10 and 11.17 pm to Penylan Road only.
Roath Park to Town Centre:
(8.00 and 8.10 am from Penylan Road only) 8.15, 8.22, 8.30 am and every 7½ min. till 10.52 pm, then 11.00 till 11.27 pm to Town Centre only.
Town Centre to Clive Road :
7.25, 7.32, 7.40 am and every 7½ min. till 11.20 pm.

Sundays

Clive Road to Town Centre and Roath Park:
2.00 pm and every 5 min. till 9.50 pm; and until 10. 20 pm to Town Centre only.
Town Centre to Roath Park:
1. 33 pm and every 5 min. till 10.08 pm.
Roath Park to Town Centre and Clive Road:
2.00 pm and every 5 min. till 9.40 pm; then until 10.20 pm to Town Centre only.
Town Centre to Clive Road :
2.12 pm and every 5 min. till 10.07 pm.

Canton and Docks Route (via Neville Street)

Clive Road to Clarence Road:
7.55 am and every 12 min. till 10.55 pm.
Clarence Road to Clive Road:
8.19 am and every 12 min. till 9.52 pm.

Sundays

Clive Road to Clarence Road:
2.00 pm and every 15 min. till 10.00 pm.
Clarence Road to Clive Road :
2.22 pm and every 15 min. till 9.52 pm.

Canton and Town Centre (Circular Route)

Clive Road to Town Centre (via Neville Street and Cardiff Bridge alternately):
7.48 am and every 6 min. till 11.10 pm.

Town Centre to Clive Road (via Neville Street and Cardiff Bridge alternately):
8.06 am and every 6 min. till 11.10 pm.

Cathedral Road and Clarence Road (via Town Centre)

Cathedral Road to Town Centre:
8.00, 8.06, 8.11 am and every 5½ min. till 11.08 pm; 11.13, 11.19, 11.25 pm to Town Centre, then to Clare Road Depot only.
Town Centre to Clarence Road:
8.11, 8.1 7, 8.22 am and every 5½ min. till 11.20 pm.
Clarence Road to Town Centre:
8.28, 8.34, 8.39 am and every 5½ min. till 10.57 pm, and until 11.19 pm to Town Centre only.
Town Centre to Cathedral Road:
8.44, 8.50, 8.55 am and every 5½ min. till 11.15 pm.

Sundays

Cathedral Road to Town Centre:
2.00 pm and every 10 min till 9.50 pm, then 10.00 and 10.10 pm to Town Centre only.
Town Centre to Clarence Road:
2.13 pm and every 10 min till 10.03 pm.
Clarence Road to Town Centre:
2.00 pm and every 10 min till 9.40 pm then 9.50 and 10.00 pm to Town Centre only.
Town Centre to Cathedral Road:
2.17 pm and every 10 min until 10.00 pm.

Cathedral Road and Docks (Direct Route)

Cathedral Road to Clarence Road:
8.40, 9.00, 9.20, 9.40 am, 1.00, 1.25, 1.55, 2.05, 4.40, 5 20, 5.30 pm.
Clarence Road to Cathedral Road :
9.00, 9.20, 9.40, 10.00 am, 12.50, 1.05, 1.30,1.45, 4.30, 5.00, 5.10, 5.40 and 6.00 pm.

Broadway (Roath) and Pier Head Route

Broadway to Pier Head:
7.45, 7.52, 7.57 and every 5 min. till 10.55 pm; 11.00, 11.10, 11.20 pm to Royal Arcade only.
Pier Head to Broadway :
8.14, 8.19, 8.24 and every 5 min. till 11.20 pm.

Sundays

Broadway to Pier Head:
1.45 pm and every 7 minutes until 9.55 pm.
Pier Head to Broadway:
2.12 pm and every 7 minutes until 10.20 pm

Penylan Road and Pier Head Route

Penylan Road to Pier Head:
8.05, 8.13, 8.21 am and every 8 min. till 10.53 pm.
Pier Head to Penylan Road:
8.37, 8.45, 8.53 am and every 8 min. till 11.12 pm; 11.19 and 11. 27 pm to Broadway, Roath.

Sundays

Roath Park to Pier Head:
2.22 pm and every 24 min. till 9.34 pm.
Pier Head to Roath Park :
2.10 pm and every 24 min. till 9.45 pm.

Cathays and Pier Head Route (via Salisbury Road)

Crwys Road to Pier Head:
8.10, 8.30, 8.50 am and every 20 min. until 10.30 pm.
Pier Head to Crwys Road:
8.40, 9.00, 9.20 am and every 20 min. until 11.00 pm.

Cathays and Town Centre Route (via Salisbury Road)

Crwys Road to Town Centre:
8.00, 8.05, 8.10 am and every 5 minutes until 11.35 pm.
Town Centre to Crwys Road:
7.40, 7.45, 7.55 am and every 5 minutes until 11.20 pm.

Sundays

Crwys Road to Town Centre:
2.10 pm and every 10 min. till 10.20 pm.
Town Centre to Crwys Road:
1.50 pm and every 10 min. till 10.00 pm.

1903 Timetables

The following are the timetables in operation on all services, including Workmen's cars, starting on 26th March, 1903 (W: Workmen's car).

Canton Section

Clive Road to Pier Head (via Cardiff Bridge):
5W20, 5W30, 6W20, 6W30, 7.30, 7.45, 7.50, 7.55,8.0 am, every 5 min. till 7.10 pm, then every 9 min. till 11.0 pm, 11.10, 11.17 to Town Centre only. Additional workmen's cars: 4.20, 5.37, 5.44 pm.
Town Centre to Pier Head:
7.46, 8.1, 8.6 am, every 5 min. till 7.26 pm, then every 9 min. till 11.16 pm.
Pier Head to Clive Road:
5W55, 6W5, 7W5, 7W15, 8.10, 8.20, 8.25 am, every 5 min. till 7 40 pm, then every 9 min. till 11.22 pm. Additional workmen's cars: 5.7, 5.12, 6.7, 6.12 pm.
Town Centre to Clive Road (via Cardiff Bridge):
7.18, 7.55, 8.2, 8.7 am, every 5 min. till 7.53 pm, then every 9 min. till 11.20, 11.28, 11.34 pm.
Clive Road to Clarence Road
5W25, 6W25, 7.40, 8.0, 8.15, 8.30, 8.45, 9.0, 9.15, 9 .30, 9.45 am, 1.12, 1.27, 1.55, 2.12 pm, 4W30, 4.30, 5.27, 5.37, 5W40, 5.40, 6.12 pm.
Clarence Road to Clive Road:
6W5, 7W15, 8.2, 8.22, 8.37, 8.52, 9.7, 9.22, 9.37 am, 12.50, 1.5, 1.35, 1.50 pm, 5.5, 5.15, 5W16, 5.50, 6.0, 6W15, 6.35 pm, then via St Mary Street every 35 min. till 11.0 p.m.
Clive Road to Wood Street:
8.16 am and every 15 min. till 10.40 pm.
Wood Street to Clive Road:
8.16 am and every 15 min. till 10.40 pm

Sundays

Clive Road to Pier Head:
2.0 pm and every 10 min. till 9 40 pm.
Pier Head to Clive Road:
2.10 pm and every 10 min. till 10.0 pm.
Clive Road to Clarence Road:
2.0 pm and every 22 min. till 9.52 pm.
Clarence Road to Clive Road:
2.0 pm and every 22 min. till 9.52 pm.

Roath Section

Broadway (Roath) to Pier Head:
5W25, 5W35, 6W25, 6W35, 7 30, 7.40, 7.45, 7 52 am, every 5 min. till 10.55, 11.0, 11.10, 11.20 pm to Royal Arcade only. Additional workmen's cars: 4.30, 4.40, 5.10, 5.35, 6.10 pm.
Pier Head to Broadway:
5W58, 6W10, 7W2, 7W12, 8.0, 8.8, 8.14, 8.19 am, every 5 min. till 11 20 pm. Additional workmen's cars: 5.10, 5.40, 6.10, 6.38 pm.
Penylan Road to Pier Head:
5W25, 5W32, 6W25. 6W32, 7.30, 7.45, 7.55, 8.2, 8.7, 8.12 am, every 5 min. till 7 30 pm, then every 9 min. till 10.55 pm, then 11.5, 11.15 pm to Royal Arcade only. Additional workmen's cars: 4.20, 5.30, 5 40 pm.
Pier Head to Penylan Road:
5W56, 6W6, 7W0, 7W10, 7.58, 8.15, 8.27, 8 .32, every 5 min. till 8.0 pm, then every 9 min. till 11.10 pm, 11.15 SO, 11.22 SO. Additional workmen's cars: 5.0, 5.10, 6.5, 6.13 pm.
Roath Park to Clive Road:
8.5, 8.15 a.m., every 9 min. till 10.45 pm.
Clive Road to Roath Park:
8.6, every 9 min. till 10.39 p.m., 10.48, 10.57 to Penylan Road only, 11.5, 11.15, 11.22, 11.30 pm to Roath. From Town Centre: 8.22 am, every 9 min., till 10.55 pm, then 11.5, and 11.15 pm to Penylan Road only.

Special Workmen's Cars

Broadway to Clive Rd.
5.25, 6.0, 6.30 (ordinary cars 7.0, 7.35 am), 5.10, 6.10 pm.
Clive Rd. to Broadway (Roath):
5.25, 6.0, 6.30 (ordinary cars 7.0, 7.35 am), 5.10, 6.0 pm.
Broadway to Grangetown via Clifton Street and Town Centre:
Broadway 5.15, 6.15.
Clifton Street 5.19, 6.19
Town Centre 5.30, 6.30.

Sundays

Broadway to Pier Head:
1.45 pm and every 7 min. till 9.55 pm.
Pier Head to Broadway
2.12 pm and every 7 min., till 10.20 pm (2.5 and 2.15 pm from Arcade only).
Roath Park to Clive Road:
2.7 pm and every 7 or 8 min. till 9.38 pm then till 10.15 pm to Arcade only. From Town Centre: 1.50 and every 7 or 8 min. till 10.4 pm.

Clive Road to Roath Park:
2.7 pm and every 7 or 8 min. till 9.52 pm, then until 10.20 to Roath. From Town Centre: 2.7 pm and every 7 or 8 min., till 10.8 pm.
Roath Park to Pier Head:
2.22 pm and every 12 min. till 9.34 pm.
Pier Head to Roath Park:
2.10 pm and every 12 min. till 9 45 pm.

Cathays Section

Crwys Road to Pier Head:
5W25, 5W30, 6W25, 6W35, 7.30, 7.40, 7.50, 8.10, 8.24, 8.32, 8.40, 8 50 am and every 20 min. till 6.50 pm. Additional workmen's cars: 4.20, 4.35, 5.35, 5.45 pm.
Pier Head to Crwys Road:
5W54, 6W8, 7W4, 7W14, 7.55, 8.10, 8.40, 9.0 am and every 20 min. till 7.25 p.m. Additional workmen's cars: 5.5, 5.15, 6.5, 6.15 pm.
Town Centre to Crwys Road
7.45 am, and every 5 min. till 8.10 am from St John Square only, 8.20 am, and every 5 min., till 11.20 pm from St Mary Street, 11.25, 11.30 pm SO.
Crwys Road to Town Centre:
8.0 am, and every 5 min. till 11.0 pm, then till 11.30 pm to St John Square only.

Sundays

Town Centre to Crwys Road:
1.53 pm and every 6½ min. till 10.7 pm.
Crwys Rd. to Town Centre:
2.0 pm and every 6½ min. till 10.25 pm.
Increased service on all routes as required.

Grangetown Section

Cathedral Road to Clarence Road (direct route):
8.40, 9.0, 9.20, 9.40 am, 1.10, 1.25, 1.55, 2.5, 4.50, 5.20, 5.30 pm.
Clarence Road to Cathedral Road
9.0, 9.20 am, 12.50, 1.5, 1.30, 1.45, 4.30, 5.5, 5.10, 5.40, 6.0 pm.

Special Cars

Cathedral Road to Pier Head via Bute Street:
7.30, 8.30, 8.50, 9.30 am.
Pier Head to Cathedral Road via Bute Street:
8.5, 8.20, 9.7 am.
Cathedral Rd. to Town Centre (via St Mary Street):
7.30, 7.45, 8.0, 8.6 am, every 5 or 6 min. until 11.13 pm, 11.19, 1125, 11 30 pm to Centre, then to Depot only.
Town Centre to Clarence Road:
7 55, 8.11 am., and every 5 or 6 min., till 11 25 pm. 11.40 pm SO.
Clarence Road to Town Centre:
8.0, 8.7, 8.14, 8.21, 8.28 am, every 5 or 6 min. till 11.2 pm, then until 11.20 pm, to Centre only.
Town Centre to Cathedral Road:
8.17, 8.24, 8.31, 8.38, 8.44 am, every 5 or 6 min. till 11.20 pm, 11.30 pm SO.

Workmen's Cars

Cathedral Road to Pier Head (via St Mary Street):
5.25, 6.25 am, 4.30, 5.35 pm.
Pier Head to Cathedral Road:
6.0, 7.7 am, 5.7, 6.7 pm.

Broadway to Clarence Road:
(Morning)

Broadway	5 15	6 15
Clifton Street	5 19	6 19
Town Centre	5 30	6 30
Clarence Road	5 44	6 44

Clarence Road to Broadway:
(Morning)

Clarence Road	5 45	6 45
Town Centre	6 1	7 1
Clifton Street	6 12	7 12
Broadway	6 16	7 16

Sundays

Cathedral Road to Town Centre:
2.0 pm and every 9 min. till 10.5 pm.
Town Centre to Clarence Road:
2.10 pm and every 9 min. till 10.7 pm.
Clarence Road to Town Centre:
2.0 pm and every 9 min. till 9.48 pm, then 9.57, 10.6 pm to Town Centre only.
Town Centre to Cathedral Road:
2.16 pm and every 9 min. till 10.3 pm.

The following is a complete list of the route indicators in use at this time, until 1913. A coloured disc to denote the route was carried under the destination indicator, on the top deck. At night, coloured lights were used.

Service	*Day*	*Night*
Clive Road & Town Centre via Neville St.	Red & White Disc	Red & White Light
Clive Road & Pier Head	Red Disc, White Cross	Green Light
Pier Head & Clive Road	Red Disc, White Cross	Red Light
Penylan Road & Pier Head	White Disc, Black Cross	White Light
Roath Park & Clive Road	Red Disc	Red Light
Broadway & Pier Head	Green Disc, White Cross	Green Light
Crwys Road & Pier Head	Yellow Disc, Black Cross	Yellow Light
Crwys Road & Town Centre	Yellow Disc	Yellow Light
Clarence Road & Cathedral Road (via Town Centre)	Blue Disc	Blue Light
Clarence Road & Cathedral Road (Direct)	Blue Disc, White Cross	-
Clarence Road & Clive Road	Red & Blue Disc	Red & Blue Light
Cathedral Road & Pier Head	White Disc, Blue Cross	-

Chapter Eighteen

Fares and Ticket Facilities

On taking over from the Tramways Company the Corporation reduced the minimum fare of 1½*d*. to 1*d*., but soon found that it was a mistake; before the Great War there were two fare increases, as fares were thought to be too low. Transfer tickets were abolished from May 1902, but a limited system of short-distance transfers was adopted in 1907, where, on payment of 1*d*., passengers could travel up to half a mile, and complete their journey, or return, by another car, the total distance not exceeding one mile. This scheme was tried out for six months, and appears to have been successful; during the first two weeks of its operation, receipts increased by £230; it tapped a new source of income, the passenger who up to now would not have bothered to make the journey at all.

In the early days, then, everybody had to pay the full fare except workmen, who could travel any distance for 1*d*., probably the cheapest workmen's fare in the country. On most routes the fare between the termini and Town Centre was 1*d*. and the cross-town fare was 2*d*.: but on the Roath Park line these fares were 2*d*. and 3*d*. respectively. Half fares for children aged from 3 to 14 were introduced on 4th December, 1922; the minimum fare was 1*d*. and 1*d*. was to be paid for an adult 2½*d*. fare. Students between the ages of 14 and 17 were also entitled to half fare tickets on production of a birth certificate, but this ruling was very soon altered and instead it became necessary to purchase a Scholar's Pass, costing one shilling.

Most fares were increased on 1st January, 1905 by one halfpenny, the hitherto maximum fare of 3*d*. (Roath Park to Clive Road, Canton) becoming 3½*d*., and the 1*d*. minimum stage being shortened. As platform staff were paid time-and-a-half for Sunday work, some councillors thought it would be a good plan to charge a 'fare-and-a-half', and even, on Bank Holidays, double fare; but this may not have been done, since legal problems may have arisen. It is believed that 'special public holiday fares', double the normal, were charged on August Bank Holiday 1906, and possibly subsequently.

A six-months trial with books of prepaid tickets at ten per cent discount started on 1st May, 1906. Each prepaid ticket was torn off in the presence of the conductor and given to him in exchange for an ordinary ticket, punched as normal. They were not allowed to be used on Sundays or Bank Holidays. The scheme was perpetuated for some time, certainly into the Great War, although most passengers seemed unaware of the facility because of lack of publicity; but it was abolished some time in the 'twenties, as R.L. Horsfield thought that a system that benefited only a section of the community was wrong in principle.

Fares were again readjusted in 1909 to iron out various anomalies; some were increased and some were reduced. After the war came another increase, of 16 per cent on the highest pre-war rates and 50 per cent on the lowest; from now until 1949 there were to be no more fare rises, but quite a few reductions.

The system of limited transfers was continued into the 'twenties; Mr Horsfield recommended against its expansion on the grounds that few

Service No. 1. GABALFA (Whitchurch Road) & CATHEDRAL ROAD (Llandaff Fields)

FARE LIST. **REVISED. In Operation, 4th October, 1932.**

SINGLE.

STAGE No.														
1		WHITCHURCH ROAD (GABALFA) (1)												
2	Fare	1d.	BANASTRE AVENUE (2)											
3	Fare	1d.	1d.	TALYGARN STREET or CANADA ROAD (3)										
4	Fare	1d.	1d.	1d.	FREE LIBRARY, FAIROAK ROAD (4)									
5	Fare	1½d.	1½d.	1d.	1d.	CRWYS ROAD (Jct. of Woodville Road) (5)								
6	Fare	1½d.	1½d.	1d.	1d.	1d.	MACKINTOSH PLACE (6)							
7	Fare	2d.	2d.	1½d.	1½d.	1d.	1d.	ST. PETER STREET (7)						
8	Fare	2d.	2d.	1½d.	1½d.	1d.	1d.	1d.	CITY ROAD (Jct. of Newport Road) (8)					
9	Fare	2d.	2d.	1½d.	1½d.	1½d.	1½d.	1d.	1d.	QUEEN STREET (Capitol) (9)				
10	Fare	2d.	2d.	2d.	2d.	1½d.	1½d.	1½d.	1d.	1d.	PARADISE PLACE (Olympia) (10)			
11	Fare	2½d.	2½d.	2d.	2d.	1½d.	1½d.	1½d.	1½d.	1d.	1d.	HIGH STREET (11)		
12	Fare	3d.	2½d.	2½d.	2½d.	2d.	2d.	2d.	1½d.	1d.	1d.	1d.	CATHEDRAL ROAD JCT. (12)	
13	Fare	3d.	3d.	3d.	3d.	2½d.	2½d.	2½d.	2d.	1½d.	1½d.	1½d.	1d.	CATHEDRAL RD. TERM. (13)

CHILDREN'S FARES.

ORDINARY.	CHILD.
1d., 1½d., 2d., 2½d.	1d.
3d.	1½d.

THROUGH TRANSFER TICKETS.

PIER HEAD and		Adult	Child
	Gabalfa via City Road	3d.	1½d.
	Crwys Road Junction via City Road	2½d.	1d.
	Cathedral Road Terminus	2½d.	1d.
	Cathedral Road Junction	2d.	1d.

Passengers Change at St. John Square or High Street.

		Adult.	Child.
Clive Street Library and Tudor Street Junction		1d.	1d.
CLIVE STREET TERMINUS and	Wood Street Junction	1½d.	1d.
	High Street or St. John Square	2d.	1d.
	Windsor Place or City Road Junction	2½d.	1d.

Passengers Change at Penarth Road Junction or Monument.

Note.—The Fare Ticket and Transfer Ticket must be presented to the Conductor of the Second Car for Cancellation.

WORKPEOPLE'S FARES: SINGLE and RETURN TICKETS are issued to all Passengers on Cars leaving Terminus between 5.0 a.m. and 7.30 a.m. only. The Return Ticket entitling the holder to make the return journey by any Car plying on same route on the day of issue between 5.0 a.m. and 11.15 p.m.

SINGLE TICKETS are also issued to Workpeople only on Special Workpeople's Cars leaving Terminus between 4.0 p.m. and 7.0 p.m. (Saturdays 12.0 noon to 2.0 p.m.).

STAGE No.	FROM		MARKET ROAD Stage No. 4.		VICTORIA PARK Stage No. 5.		CATHEDRAL RD. JCT. Stage No. 6.		MONT. (St. Mary St.) Stage No. 7.		CATHEDRAL RD. TERMS. Stage No. 8.		PIER HEAD Stage No. 9.	
			SINGLE.	RETURN.	SINGLE.	RETURN.	SINGLE.	RETURN.	SINGLE.	RETURN.	SINGLE.	RETURN.	SINGLE.	RETURN.
1	WHITCHURCH RD. (Gabalfa)	Fare	1½d.	3d.	2d.	4d.	1d.	2d.	1d.	2d.	1½d.	3d.	1½d.	3d.
2	CRWYS RD. (Jct. of Woodville Road)	Fare	1d.	2d.	1½d.	3d.	—	—	—	—	1d.	2d.	—	—
3	CITY RD. (Jct. of Newport Road)	Fare	—	—	1d.	2d.	—	—	—	—	—	—	1d.	2d.

TRANSFER TICKETS WITH WORKPEOPLE'S RETURN FARES.

In addition to the Cheap Return Fares for Workpeople at present in operation on Cars making direct Services, THROUGH RETURN TICKETS will be issued enabling the passenger to travel either way over the section shewn on separate Fare Lists by transferring to ANY CAR on the various Services for the desired destination.

Central Offices, Paradise Place, Cardiff, May, 1935.

WILLIAM FORBES, General Manager and Engineer.

Priory Press Ltd., The Friary, Cardiff. 40775

Service No. 2.—Pengam Bridge, Newport Road and Pier Head.

FARE LIST. REVISED. In Operation 4th October, 1932.

SINGLE.

STAGE No.															
1		PENGAM BRIDGE (1)													
2	Fare	1d.	ROYAL OAK, NEWPORT ROAD (2)												
3	Fare	1d.	1d.	PRIEST ROAD (3)											
4	Fare	1d.	1d.	1d.	CLIFTON STREET (4)										
5	Fare	1½d.	1½d.	1d.	1d.	CITY ROAD JUNCTION (5)									
6	Fare	1½d.	1½d.	1½d.	1d.	1d.	132 QUEEN STREET (Capitol) (6)								
7	Fare	2d.	2d.	1½d.	1½d.	1d.	1d.	PARADISE PLACE (Olympia) (7)							
8	Fare	2d.	2d.	2d.	1½d.	1½d.	1d.	1d.	HIGH STREET (8)						
9	Fare	2½d.	2½d.	2½d.	2d.	1½d.	1d.	1d.	1d.	ANGEL HOTEL (9)					
10	Fare	2½d.	2½d.	2½d.	2d.	1½d.	1d.	1d.	1d.	1d.	CATHEDRAL ROAD JUNCTION (10)				
11	Fare	3d.	3d.	3d.	2½d.	2d.	1½d.	1½d.	1d.	1d.	1d.	WYNDHAM CRESCENT (11)			
12	Fare	3d.	3d.	3d.	2½d.	2d.	1½d.	1½d.	1½d.	1½d.	1d.	1d.	MARKET ROAD (12)		
13	Fare	3½d.	3d.	3d.	3d.	2½d.	2d.	2d.	2d.	1½d.	1½d.	1½d.	1d.	BEDA ROAD (13)	
14	Fare	3½d.	3d.	3d.	3d.	2½d.	2d.	2d.	2d.	2d.	1½d.	1½d.	1d.	1d.	VICTORIA PARK (14)
15	Fare	2d.	2d.	2d.	1½d.	1½d.	1d.	1d.	ST. JOHN SQUARE (15)						
16	Fare	2d.	2d.	2d.	1½d.	1½d.	1d.	1d	1d.	HAYES BRIDGE or MONUMENT (16)					
17	Fare	2½d.	2½d.	2½d.	2½d.	2d.	2d.	1½d.	1½d.	1d.	SOPHIA STREET (17)				
18	Fare	2½d.	2½d.	2½d.	2½d.	2½d.	2d.	2d.	1½d.	1½d.	1d.	PIER HEAD (18)			

Service No. 2.

	EITHER WAY
Stage 20. Clive Rd. and Wyndham Cres.	1d.
Stage 21. Stacey Road and City Rd. Jctn.	1d.

CHILDREN'S FARES.	
ORDINARY.	CHILD.
1d., 1½d., 2d., 2½d.	1d.
3d., 3½d.	1½d.

THROUGH TRANSFER TICKETS.

	Adult	Child.
PIER HEAD and Pengam	2½d.	1d.

Passengers change at St. John Square, Hayes Bridge or High Street.

	Adult	Child.
Clive Street Library and Tudor Street Junction	1d.	1d.
CLIVE STREET TERMINUS and Wood Street Junction	1½d.	1d.
CLIVE STREET TERMINUS and St. John Square or High Street	2d.	1d.
CLIVE STREET TERMINUS and Windsor Place or City Road Junction	2½d.	1d.

Passengers change at Penarth Road Junction or Monument.

NOTE.—The Fare Ticket and Transfer Ticket must be presented to the Conductor of the Second Car for cancellation.

WORKPEOPLE'S FARES { SINGLE AND RETURN TICKETS are issued to all passengers on Cars leaving Terminus between 5.0 a.m. and 7.30 a.m. only. The Return Ticket, entitling the holder to make the return journey by any Car plying on the same route on the day of issue between 5.0 a.m. and 11.15 p.m. SINGLE TICKETS are also issued to Workpeople only on Special Workpeople's Cars leaving Terminus between 4.0 p.m. and 7.0 p.m. (Saturdays 12.0 noon to 2.0 p.m.)

STAGE No.	FROM		MARKET ROAD Stage No. 12		VICTORIA PARK Stage No. 14		HAYES B. or MONT. Stage No. 16		PIER HEAD Stage No. 18	
			SINGLE	RETURN	SINGLE	RETURN	SINGLE	RETURN	SINGLE	RETURN
1	PENGAM BRIDGE (Newport Road)	Fare	1d.	2d.	1½d.	3d.	1d	2d.	1½d.	3d.
5	CITY ROAD (Junction of Newport Road)	Fare	—	—	1d.	2d.	—	—	1d.	2d.

TRANSFER TICKETS WITH WORKPEOPLE'S RETURN FARES.

In addition to the Cheap Return Fares for Workpeople at present in operation on Cars making direct Services, THROUGH RETURN TICKETS will be issued enabling the passengers to travel either

JK5839
WORKPEOPLES' TICKET
Victoria P. Terminus
Cathedral Road Ter
Clarence Road Terminus
Neville St Junction
Hamilton Street
WoodStreet Junction
Tudor St. Junction
Splott Terminus
T. V. R. Stn Queen St
Pier Head
Cathedral Rd Junc
FARE 1d
Cardiff City Tramways & Motors.
Issued subject to Bye-laws. Available on one Car to Station OPPOSITE punch-hole.
Ticket must be given up on demand
Roath Park Terminus
Penylan Rd Terminus
Crwys Road Junction
Lowther Road
Clive Street Grange
Whitchurch Road Ter
City Road Junction
Newport Rd Terminus
Fitzalan Road
Hayes Bridge
Monument
Market Road
Bell Punch Co., Uxbridge. 10-24

AZ 4644
CARDIFF CITY TRAMWAYS AND MOTORS.
Fare 1d. either way.
IN 1 2 3 4 5 6 7 8
OUT 1 2 3 4 5 6 7 8
Issued subject to Bye-laws. Available on Station opposite punch-hole. To be shown on demand.
Bell Punch Co., Uxbridge 9-23

WD 0276
A. B. C. D. J. ROUTES.
Whitchurch Road
Splott Terminus
City Road Junction
Newport Rd Terminus
Carlisle Street
P[illegible] Place
Priest Road
Sophia Street
St. John's Square
WORK-PEOPLE
FARE 1½d
CARDIFF CITY TRAMWAYS & MOTORS
Issued subject to Bye-laws. Available on one Car to Station OPPOSITE punch-hole.
Must be given up on demand.
Pier Head
Fair Oak Road
Penylan Road
CornrCity & AlbanyRd
T. V. R. Stn Queen St
Windsor Place
Crwys Road Junction
Clifton Street
Monument
Hayes Bdge orRoyalA
Bell Punch Co., Uxbridge 7-24

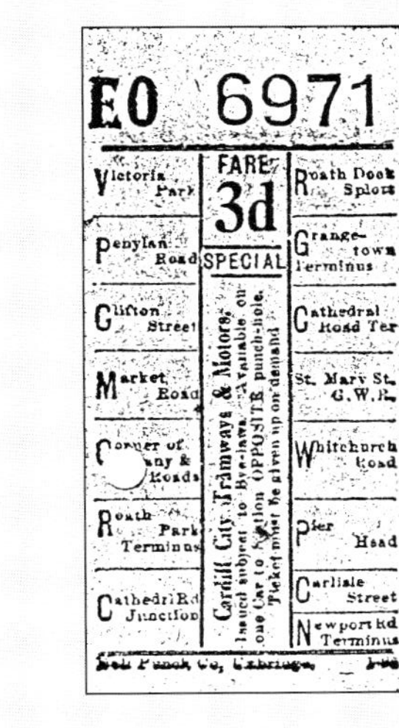

A selection of tickets.

IW 9588
F. G. I ROUTES.
Victoria Park
Penarth Rd Junction
Cathedral Road
Tudor St Junction
Fitzalan Road
Splott Terminus
WoodStreet Junction
WORK-PEOPLE
FARE 1½d
CARDIFF CITY TRAMWAYS & MOTORS
Issued subject to Bye-laws. Available on one Car to Station OPPOSITE punch-hole.
Must be given up on demand.
Pier Head
Market Road
Angel Hotel
Beda Road
Grange-town
Clare Gardens
Carlisle Street
High [illegible]
Monument
Bell Punch Co., Uxbridge.

XT 5365
Newport Rd Terminus
Roath Park
Corner of Albany & City Roads
Crwys Road Junction
Penylan Rd Terminus
Market Road
Whitchurch Road
Victoria Park Terminus
Cathedral Rd Junction
Clifton Street
FARE 2½d
SPECIAL
CARDIFF CITY TRAMWAYS & MOTORS
Issued subject to Bye-laws. Available on one Car to Station OPPOSITE punch-hole.
Ticket must be given up on demand.
Cathedral Rd Terminus
Clarence Rd Terminus
Grange-town Terminus
Carlisle Street
St. John Square
Pier Head
Wood Street
Hayes Bridge or Monument
High Street
Roath Dock Splott
Bell Punch Co.

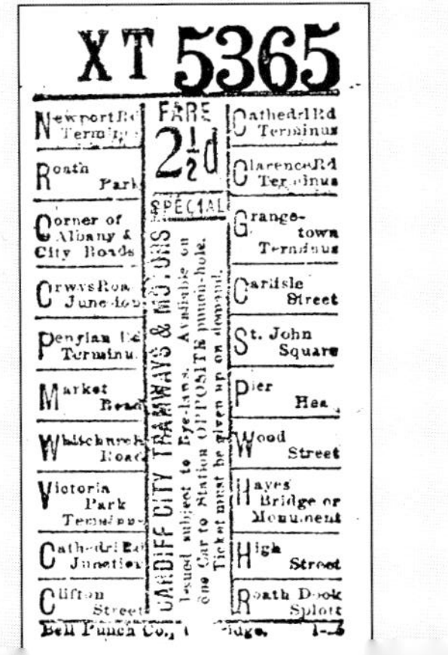

passengers would benefit. Workmen's cars were still running, as usual at a loss, and when the new bus services started they had no workmen's fares since there was no statutory obligation to provide them. It was thought desirable to have combined car and bus tickets for transfer at Victoria Park and Newport Road to the new feeder buses; and in 1928 the General Manager introduced a new return ticket, to relieve conductors of extra work and to reduce the ticket stock required.

The fare from Newport Road to Victoria Park was reduced from 3½*d*. to 3*d*. and that from City Road junction from 3*d*. to 2½*d*. in 1929. Transfer tickets were issued on this service (No. 2A) to enable passengers to travel to the Docks; and from Splott a 3*d*. transfer was available for workmen travelling to Pier Head. A new system of workmen's transfer returns was innovated in 1930 by William Forbes. The ticket, issued up to 7.30 am only, was limited to travel by two cars only on the forward and return journeys, and in the forward journey available for completion of the second journey up to 8.15 am only. For the return journey, the ticket was available at any time on day of issue. This scheme obviated running an excessive number of cars during the 'rush'.

The maximum fare was 4*d*., used only on the through Roath Park-Victoria Park service, more than four miles in length. For other services, 3½*d*. was the maximum, and 2*d*. the in-town fare, e.g. Whitchurch Road to St Mary Street.

By 1934 transfer facilities had become quite extensive; in a local guidebook* William Forbes wrote:

> Fares have been readjusted and cheapened in numerous instances. In connection with the services operating internally, both on buses and cars, the readjusted and cheapened fares have been offered through the medium of Transfer Tickets, such Transfer Tickets being available from bus to bus, or bus to car, or vice versa. The transfer facilities have necessitated only one cash transaction to be made in place of the four which would be necessary with a return journey and change of two vehicles. The public has benefited from transfers, and increased traffic has resulted.

When Service 12 was diverted from Clive Street Grange to Clarence Road, a further crop of transfers was instigated for Grangetown passengers, who thus continued to enjoy through bookings as before, even without through cars:

Transfers over Service No. 7

Clive Street Library and Tudor Street Junction	1*d*.
Clive Street Terminus and Wood Street Junction	1½*d*.
Clive Street Terminus and High Street and St John Square	2*d*.
Clive Street Terminus and City Road Junction	2½*d*.

Transfer could be made at Penarth Road Junction for Services 6 and 12, or at the Monument for all tram services via Queen Street or bus services 39 and 40 as far as Windsor Place. On journeys to Clive Street, travel could be made on any tram or bus via Queen Street to the Monument, where transfer was to be made.

Further transfer facilities were introduced in 1936: Cathedral Road and

* From *The City, Port and District of Cardiff*, published by The Western Mail & Echo Ltd, 1933.

Clarence Road (change in Town Centre to No. 12); Cathedral Road and Roath Park, Newport Road, Splott or Whitchurch Road (change in Town Centre); Whitchurch Road and Victoria Park (change in Town Centre). A new workmen's transfer return, 3*d.*, was available between Roath Park, Newport Road, Whitchurch Road, Roath Dock and Penarth Road Junction, change to be made in Town Centre.

The tramways were now more prosperous than at any previous period of their history; the 1939 fare reductions indicated that much, and by 1940, with just 1*d.* and 1½*d.* fares, revenue increased by about £500 a week; between 1st April and 4th May of that year there were 4,030,392 passengers, compared with 2,391,451 over the same period in 1939. The revolutionary Pay-as-you-Enter system has been described; the special 3*d.* souvenir tickets issued on the last day were the first since 1943 - and the last.

Tickets themselves were the usual Bell Punch type, the machines remaining the property of the Bell Punch Company; the hire charge was 15 shillings a year for each punch, reduced to 12*s.* in 1907. The company also had advertising rights on the ticket backs, in return for a reduction in price of the tickets.

The Eastern Routes tickets were headed 'A B C D J Routes', and the Western ones 'F G I Routes', even after service numbers were introduced; the letters corresponded to Nos. 1, 2, 3, 4, 8 and 5, 6, 7 respectively.

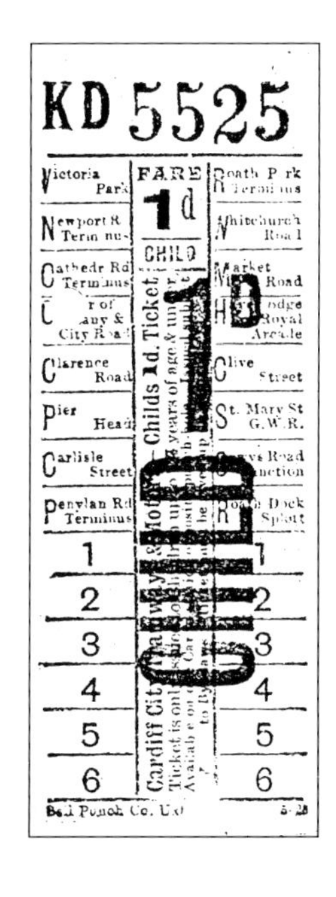

Chapter Nineteen

Operating Practices

Where two cars met on a single line, the rule was that the car nearer a loop must turn back; but incidents like this were not supposed to happen at all, and a report had to be made out if they did.

The 1905 Rulebook stated;

During wet and stormy weather, and times of heavy traffic, 6 are to be allowed to stand inside the 4-wheel double deck cars, 9 passengers inside the double deck bogie cars, and 12 passengers inside the single deck cars, after all the seats are occupied.

Dogs were not allowed aboard trams generally.

Bell signal code from Conductor to Motorman was as follows:

1 - Stop, 2 - Start, 3 - Stop quickly, 4 - Car full.

And from Motorman to Conductor:

1 - Throw in automatic switch, 2 - Attend to trolley, 2 - Put on the rear brake, 4 - Come and speak.

If the tram was running three or more minutes late, a written report, giving reasons, had to be made out . . . but this was in 1905. An amazing amount of equipment was carried by each car in service: pair of rubber gloves, towing rope, 2 screwdrivers, hammer, chisel, pinchbar, length of insulated cable, shifting spanner, pair of pliers, supply of fuses, a lifting jack and handle.

It was the practice at Cardiff for cars berthed in the depot to have the trolley pole off the wire, the main switches, controller and reversing handle off, and the handbrake left on. Had there been a fire, it would certainly have been impossible to get the cars out of the shed quickly.

At 4 mph speed restriction over all facing points was in force, and cars were not to pass on curves. Cathedral Road was one of the fastest sections of the system in 1905, a maximum speed of 14 mph being allowed.

Generally speaking, cars were not designed for specific services, except the single deckers. In the early 'twenties, Service 6 was worked entirely by 4-wheelers, and, after the introduction of the top-covered cars, the vestibuled bogie open-toppers usually worked the Sundays Only Service 9, Roath Park and Victoria Park, particularly in summer. The new Brush single-deck cars worked on both Services 1 and 7, and sometimes on the others, except No. 6.

Conclusion

Cardiff's tramways, throughout their life, were run as ruthlessly and efficiently as any privately-owned business; and the dictum employed down the years was that if a facility did not pay, eliminate it. The tramways were always self-sufficient, *never* subsidised from rates, in fact they contributed huge sums to relief of rates, and generally managed to make a profit. (A loss was made in 1927, 1931, 1934 and 1937.) It was clearly one of the most successful transport undertakings in Britain; and there is no doubt that Cardiff was very much the poorer once the last tram had run into the depot on the 20th February, 1950.

Cardiff's last tram - decorated car No. 11 turns from St Mary Street into Custom House Street on 20th February, 1950. The verse on the side reads:

To all you old timers - and you still in your teens
Who rode with me through years of war - packed in just like sardines
I'd like to thank you one and all for the patience you have shown
And say Farewell to the finest folk that a tram has ever known

Ian L. Wright

Appendix One

The Cardiff-Penarth Tramway Proposal

The idea of a tramway linking Cardiff with nearby Penarth seems to have been first mentioned in January 1903, when a Cardiff alderman commented that Penarth was welcome to build a tramway up to the boundary and Cardiff would then build one to the boundary to link up with it. What he did not favour was 'running any risks' with a jointly-owned line. And any such notions were successfully resisted by Cardiff, who never did have any jointly-owned tramways, although there were in later years joint bus routes.

In November 1903, the Penarth Tramway Syndicate, whose plans were almost completed, were ready to apply for a Provisional Order. The line, which would be single with passing places, would run from Grangetown Bridge to Penarth Post Office; a dangerous part of road at Cogan Hill would have to be widened, and the part of the road owned by Lord Bute be purchased, bringing the estimated cost of the scheme to £100,000. The Syndicate expressed the hope that the support and co-operation of both Cardiff and Penarth councils would be gained.

The cost of taking over Penarth Road, widening it, constructing the bridges and tramway was by December reckoned to be between £150,000 and £250,000. The proposal was that the line would join the Corporation's system at Clive Street. Dinas Powis Parish Council received a plan showing that a branch line would be laid through Eastbrook and terminate at a new hotel on the main road from Dinas Powis. This council decided to favour the Bill. Total length of the main line plus branch was to be 4 miles 26 chains.

However, a suspicious Cardiff Council decided to oppose the scheme; it had been reported that 'the ulterior object of the syndicate was to enter into competition with the Cardiff Corporation Tramways.' But the Penarth Tramway Syndicate insisted that their line must be beneficial not only to outer districts, but to Cardiff as well.

In January 1904 the Syndicate had also reached deadlock with Penarth Urban District Council, the former optimistically believing that if the Penarth ratepayers were appealed to they would unanimously support the scheme. The Council had made several amendments to the Bill, and the promoters were unwilling to accept all of them; even so, many concessions were made, and it is indeed astounding the lengths they were prepared to go to get the line open. Being unable to lay a double line, they would place loops at frequent intervals and have a signalman between them where it was not possible to see from one loop to the other. They would widen Cogan Hill to fifty feet; erect iron girders to widen and strengthen Ely bridge, even though it was just as strong as Taff bridge, over which Cardiff trams ran. The promoters were prepared to purchase at least 50 per cent of their current from the Penarth Electric Light Co.; to extend the Penarth tram terminus to Windsor Terrace; to lay the entire line in wood blocks; and to contribute thousands of pounds to freeing the Penarth toll-gate.

Four years later no further progress had been made. *Railways and Tramways* for April 1908 reported that the Penarth Tramway Syndicate (Messrs Vachell & Co. of Cardiff) had asked Penarth District Council's consent to build a Penarth-Cardiff tramway and that the council had asked the syndicate to agree to 'certain stipulated conditions'. Clearly, the council was putting off the awful day when it might actually have to say 'yes' - or 'no'.

With Penarth's unreasonable demands, and Cardiff's firm opposition, it is certainly not surprising that the Cardiff-Penarth line was never built. Had it been, no doubt traffic would have built up, and the Taff Vale Railway's Penarth branch would have lost a good deal, but it is doubtful whether it would have survived the 1930s.

Appendix Two

Some Tramway Memories

The following reminiscences of the Cardiff tramways were written in 1987 by Sid Rickard, and they are included here with his kind permission. He lived in Cardiff from 1922 until the 1950s and his recollections are particularly strong of the Crwys Road-Albany Road-City Road area.

My first interesting sight was in about 1925, at the age of five, when one of the new single deckers was turning off Crwys Road into Woodville Road. I think it must have been No. 53, as it would have been a bit early for any of the others to have been delivered.

I can't remember ever seeing any of the rebuilt open-top cars on the Roath Park line after the new covered-top cars had been delivered in quantity, but for some reason they did survive on the Whitchurch Road line to a much later date, particularly in the peak periods. I remember seeing one of the rebuilt cars coming down Crwys Road around 5.50 pm one day in 1930, displaying half of the route number '1' on the indicator and the single word 'Splott' on the destination blind, instead of the usual 'Roath Dock Splott'. The practice of displaying half of No. 1 (the top half being the bottom portion of the blank blind) was quite common on this route for any car that was not making the full journey, or was departing from the normal No. 1 route.

In the 1920s and even the 1930s Roath Park was a meeting place for people from all parts of Cardiff. In summer it was a hive of activity with many thousands of people either swimming, boating, or listening to band concerts and choirs. It had to be seen to be believed. Therefore there was every justification to lay a tramway in Marlborough Road to give a direct connection from the Broadway area to Roath Park. In addition it would have provided a more direct route for first and last cars to or from the depot and Roath Park and Penylan Road. After firework displays there would be a dozen or more cars at around 11.00 pm waiting to traverse the Roath Park circle and go to all parts of Cardiff.

One day in 1928/9 I managed to extract twopence from my father so that my brother and I could take a Sunday afternoon car from Roath Park to Victoria Park. I suppose that I was fairly well behaved as a lad, but on the way back in a Brush car, whilst sitting up front on the top deck, I could not resist slyly and slowly altering the route number display by turning the handle. When we reached the city centre I heard the conductor storming up the stairs, the money jingling in his bag. A boarding passenger had told him that his route number was wrong. The conductor certainly was not very pleased, and gave us a telling-off.

As a boy I often wondered about the long length of deserted track that led into the former horse-tram depot at Cathays. It must have survived until about 1930, although latterly the actual pointwork in Crwys Road was removed.

It was rare for a tram's trolley to dewire. At many junctions the trolley operated the overhead frog in a simple and effective way. A diverging car's trolley would hit a vertical bar suspended from the frog and give it a quick flip, which would alter the frog just long enough for the trolley wheel to pass over, the frog then returning to its normal position. At the most important junctions the points were operated by the car passing a point short of the junction either with power on or power off. Usually it was successful, but it didn't always work and the driver then had to get out the point-iron.

The overhead frog at Penylan Road was, however, manually operated. At the junction

pole was a box mounted some six feet above the ground, and a lever projected out of its side. I remember a woman conductor jumping off the car, leaping up and hanging on to the lever until the trolley passed over, then running after the car and jumping on as it entered Penylan Road. It was quite an athletic performance. Incidentally, Penylan Road was the only terminus that had a facing crossover.

I remember the signals protecting the Heathfield Road-Maitland Street single-line section when they were new in 1928. They were of a rather peculiar design; the arm was rather short, but quite deep. When the arm was in the danger position it obscured a large white (or green) light and exposed a similar red light below. When the arm went to the clear position it covered the red light and exposed the other light above. However, in later days they fell out of use and the drivers went through when they thought the track was clear.

One misty day in 1949 an inward-bound car had just left the Maitland Street loop as a northbound car entered the single line at Heathfield Road. The northbound car could not reverse on to the double track as the spring-loaded points would have landed it on the inward-bound track. So the car at the Maitland Street end had to reverse right through the loop and then come forward on to the inward side of the loop to allow the northbound car to pass. The car at Maitland Street again came forward on to the single line section when *another* northbound car entered the single line at Heathfield Road. The southbound car had once more to reverse through the Maitland Street loop, allow the other car to pass, and then come on to the single line section for the third time. This time it got through!

About 1948 or 1949 Cardiff experienced a terrible storm, and the rain soaked into the wood blocks with which some of the streets were paved and they started to swell. Eventually they began popping out of the tracks all over the place, both in the city and at the termini. The Roath Park route was reduced to operating from Penylan Road to City Road Junction. At about 7.00 pm I was standing at the stop at the bottom of City Road waiting for a tram; eventually one came down from Penylan Road and went through the trailing crossover before reversing to return north. However, all couldn't have been well with the points. The driver and the conductor looked at them, and then the driver went and obtained the point-iron and stuck it into the points almost horizontally. The driver then brought the car forward and, as it got to the points, the observing conductor shouted 'Roll'er,' and the tram lurched over on to the crossover without much ado. By the casual way the operation was carried out I should say that it was not all that rare a procedure.

During this period, 1946-50, there were several short workings. At City Road Junction passengers for Roath Park and Whitchurch Road stood no chance of boarding cars that had come from the city in the evening peak, as the cars were full by the time they reached the junction. Extra cars were sent out from Newport Road depot, via Glossop Road, for Whitchurch Road and Roath Park. I also recall a lunchtime extra from Whitchurch Road to Adamsdown Square, and presumably it went back to the depot from there.

Although the cars were rather run-down, their rough riding was due solely to the track, particularly in Ninian Road. When these cars were diverted off the normal route through Queen Street and on to the relatively unused Adam Street line they still ran very sweetly indeed over that section.

* * * * * * * *

Ian L. Wright is another who loved the trams of Cardiff. From November 1938 he had the good fortune to live in a house on Whitchurch Road that overlooked the Maitland Street passing loop and from that time on the trams

began to make an impact on his life. There were very few local tramway enthusiasts, but it was a group of four, comprising Mr Wright, Robert W.A. Jones, Derek Chaplin and Geoffrey Booth (all members of the Light Railway Transport League) who were instrumental in saving the water car from oblivion; and a few small fittings from the top-covered cars were rescued too. Mr Wright also saved a 1913 enamel route number plate 'Service No. 5' and eventually presented it to the Welsh Industrial and Maritime Museum. Here are some of Ian Wright's recollections.

My first memory of the Cardiff trams was of 1932, somewhere near Tresillian Terrace in the Penarth Road. One of the long, low, single-deck cars with the rattan cane seats emerged from under the railway bridge and clattered over the points, adding a touch of dignity to downtown Cardiff on the line from Splott to Grangetown. Those cars did barely ten years' work in Cardiff before being sold to Brazil in 1940. What a waste!

Then there were pre-war Bank Holiday rides from Roath Park to Victoria Park on breezy open-top bogie trams that Cardiff kept for special occasions. Those cars growled their sedate way over Cardiff Bridge like ocean liners, the enamelled advertisements along their sides announcing BOVRIL and HEINZ SPAGHETTI, and we hurried down off the car at Victoria Park in time to visit the lake and watch Billy the Seal.

The trams were there too at the Pier Head to take us home as we crowded off the Campbell paddle steamers from holidays at Weston, Minehead, or Ilfracombe. How did the white-capped summer conductors cope with all those passengers' fares, I wondered?

Whitchurch Road was paved in wood blocks as far as the Talygarn Street crossover - the remnant of the old terminus (the extension was laid in mastic asphalt). Drivers always careered through this crossover at a fair old lick on their way to and from Gabalfa terminus and there was a good deal of noise and lurching as the trailing points were hit. On Palm Sunday extra cars used the crossover when people came to Cathays cemetery to put flowers on the graves. I think the practice must have stopped after the War. The water car often used it on Sunday morning, railgrinding right up to 1949.

Cardiff is a very rainy city, and after one deluge in the 1940s I remember vividly seeing in Newport Road, near the junction with Marlborough Road, nearly a foot of water with the tramway wood blocks floating about all over the place. Another sight was that of fountains of water shooting up out of the pointwork at places such as St John Square/Queen Street junction whenever the automatic points were slotted into position in advance of approaching tramcars. On wet days it could be quite spectacular!

By the late 1930s the ten bogie open-top tramcars which had been rebuilt and retained after the original fleet of 1902-built cars was replaced were not often seen except at times of pressure and at Bank Holidays, when they were sent out to deal with the crowds. They made their way sedately down City Road and Newport Road with a gentle rolling motion, the bogie wheels picking out a four-beat percussion over the rail joints - 'tap tap, tap tap' - a sound that had become rare in Cardiff streets since the withdrawal of most of the bogie cars from regular service in 1936.

Some special occasions live in the memory. On Saturday, 10th June, 1939, when I was 12 and living on the Whitchurch Road tram route I was amazed to see three open-top bogie cars, Nos. 22, 30 and 84, arriving at the Gabalfa terminus during the afternoon. Perhaps some unusual event was on in Cardiff that day. Maybe the cars had come up from the Pier Head after moving the crowds from a P. & A. Campbell paddle steamer sailing in the Bristol Channel. Whatever it was, the arrival of these cars was unusual enough for it to have been noted down in my schoolboy diary. During the 12 years I lived on the tram route I never saw a car of this type on Whitchurch Road again.

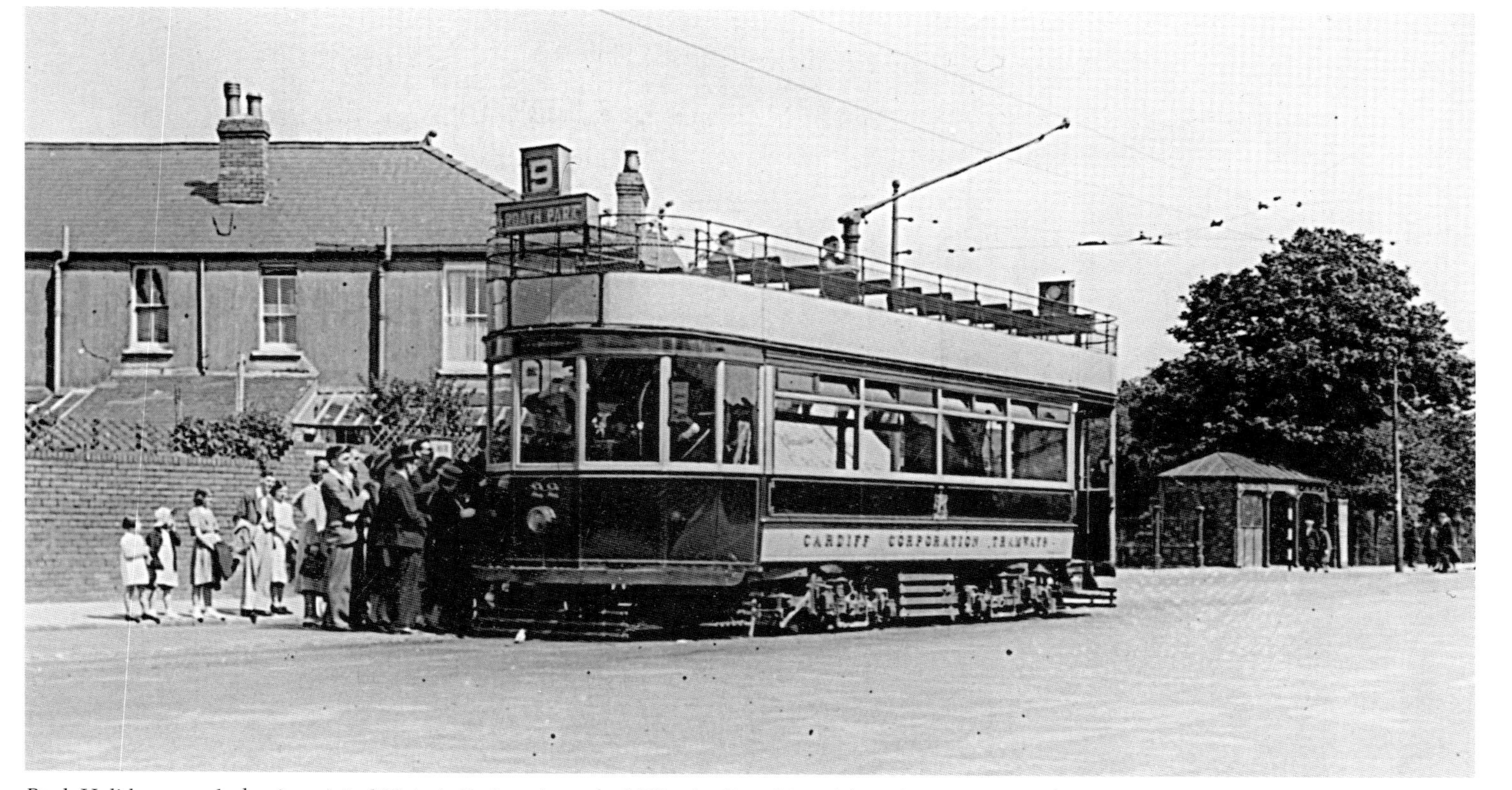

Bank Holiday crowds, having visited Victoria Park and watched Billy the (female) seal, board car No. 22 for the return journey on service 9 to Roath Park, 7th August, 1939. The trolley has yet to be turned by the automatic reverser, visible above right.

H.B. Priestley

The bogie open toppers gave pleasure to hundreds when they appeared on route 9 on pre-war summer Sundays. The long ride from Roath Park to Victoria Park was very popular in the days of simpler pleasures and there was much competition to get the top-deck seats. On Good Friday, 7th April, 1939, I made the journey in both directions on car No. 32. From the windswept top deck the sights and sounds were unforgettable; the colourful flower baskets on the tramway standards in Duke Street, the view of Cardiff Castle and the crossing of Cardiff Bridge. I remember too the voices of excited children, the growl of the tramcar's motors and the clatter over the points. There were rather alarming moments too as the car headed for the low girders of the Queen Street railway bridges and everyone instinctively ducked. The overhead trolley pole, pressed down to almost a horizontal position, flashed blue sparks from its wheel on the wires.

In 1946 Nos. 22 and 84 could still be seen doing rush hour turns on the Victoria Park route with their fenders still bearing traces of wartime white paint, the cars being equipped with Pay As You Enter flat-fare boxes. On 13th August, 1946, I made a final journey across Cardiff on the top deck of No. 84 accompanied by tramway enthusiast Fred Ward. It must have been very near the end for those wonderful old cars with their coachwork still immaculate through long hours spent in the depot. Later that year they were taken to Clare Road depot for breaking up.

A Derailment Remembered. - On 19th October, 1948, I was at home in Whitchurch Road when I was startled by a sound like thunder from the street outside. Standard car No. 40 was just coming off the Maitland Street loop when it became derailed almost outside my house, finishing up a few feet from the kerb and completely blocking the road. I rushed for my camera and recorded the unusual scene. It was the first time I had seen a tramcar off the track.

Normal service was resumed after about 15 minutes when a following car was commandeered. This coupled up to No. 40 and drew it back on to the rails.

Derailments were frequent in the post-war years of neglect, for the rail-head was so worn as to be nearly profile-less. Here, in Whitchurch Road on the single-line section opposite Flaxland Avenue (and right outside the photographer's home), car No. 40 has made itself unpopular with road-users on 19th October, 1948. *Ian L. Wright*

On a Sunday morning a few weeks later the maintenance gang turned up. Gwilym, the CCT's square and stocky welder, hooked a power line on to the overhead wire and the length of rail was laid bare, lifted out and a new one inserted. There was little traffic about in those austere days, and the only warning of the hole in the road was two red flags on that Sunday morning in 1948.

The Last Tram to Roath Park. - On Saturday night, 3rd December, 1949, four Light Railway Transport League members, myself included, gave the last car, No. 107, a rousing send-off, and helped to add gaiety to an occasion which would normally have remained inconspicuous. We showed up an unenterprising Transport Department by decorating the car ourselves and provided souvenir tramcar gongs and motor horns which we put to good use. We hoped that our efforts would influence a parsimonious Finance Committee to provide some sort of ceremony for the last Cardiff car to Whitchurch Road in February 1950.

Cardiff's trams had seemed to be as permanent a part of the city as the Great Western Railway or the Empire Cinema, and Queen Street seemed unthinkable without them; but they were gone. *Sic transit gloria.*

One of the Cardiff tramway enthusiasts mentioned earlier was Geoffrey Booth. His contribution to preserving the memory of the tramcar was to shoot dozens of feet of film between December 1949 and February 1950 showing trams in action in several locations; when completed he joined all the sections of film in the correct order to make one reel with a running time of twenty minutes. The film itself was 9.5 mm, with central slots; black and white, without sound.

Tramcars were shown at Roath Park, Bute Terrace, St Mary Street, Custom House Street, Roath depot, Crwys Road, Moira Terrace, Whitchurch Road and City Road junction. A car was shown using the crossover in Newport Road after coming out of Glossop Road; another car was shown using the automatic trolley reverser at Whitchurch Road terminus. The decorated last car, No. 11, was featured. The viewer could observe that quite high speeds were attained on the Adam Street section with its excellent track; but on the bad sections of track the cars pitched alarmingly. Cars Nos. 71, 11 and 113 featured in the film.

It was the only amateur-made film known showing the Cardiff trams and, after Geoffrey Booth's death a few years ago, it is believed the film went to the Tramway Museum Society.

A Cardiff tram features very briefly in the opening scene of the 1943 film *The Halfway House* (starring Mervyn Johns and Tom Walls). It is merely a scene-setting shot headed 'Cardiff' and shows a car passing the castle.

Appendix Three

Highfield Electric Tramway

Electric traction returned to Cardiff in a small way in 1973 when the Whitchurch (Cardiff) & District Model Engineering Society, which had a small plot of land adjacent to Heath Junction (where the old Cardiff Railway diverged from the Rhymney Railway), opened a short length of 18 in.-gauge tramway.

Old colliery rails were used, and the track took two days to be laid during November 1972. All pointwork was made on site. The single line, with a branch leading to a small shed, ran parallel with the Cardiff Railway, the termini being designated Northend and Southend. In the shed a 3½ hp single-phase ex-organ AC motor, with magnetic overload cutout, generated direct current at 45-49 volts, 48 volts being the normal voltage for the traction supply. The motor generator worked off the mains supply.

There was one tramcar, a 4-wheel crossbench type seating ten passengers. No. 1 was designed and built by Felix Cunuder, who had been engineer and rolling stock superintendent with Cardiff Corporation Transport Department from 1947 and finally Deputy General Manager and engineer until about 1970. The car's underframe was built at Mr Cunuder's home but the body was made at Highfield, assisted by a society member known only as 'Squeaky' Spriggs. No. 1 was powered by a single motor; a pair of cut-down BTH B510 controllers, ex-Cardiff Corporation Tramways, were fitted and the controller contacts were mounted under one of the seats. Working headlights were fitted, and braking was by hand. No. 1 was roofed and canopied but was otherwise open-sided, and the livery was pale green.

Opening day of the line was 26th May, 1973, and the Lord Mayor of Cardiff, Alderman Turnbull, drove the tram on that occasion. Subsequently the tramway was open to the public only on Bank Holidays, as was the associated live-steam passenger-carrying miniature railway.

In 1977 a second line was added so that there was now virtually double track for most of the way, with single-line terminal stubs, the north terminus now being equipped with an automatic trolley reverser.

A second tram was built in 1981, and again it was entirely original in concept, not in any way a 'model' of any type of car that had run in Britain. It was a bogie car, 20 ft long, with 20 seats in a curious semi-enclosed, semi-open body; the enclosed half of the body was fully glazed. Two 50-75 volt motors powered the car, and again there were two ex-Cardiff Corporation BTH B510 controllers that had been rescued years before from one of the Brush top-covered cars. No. 2 had air-wheel brakes, roller-bearing axleboxes, and the bogie wheels were 1 ft in diameter.

Unfortunately the land on which the Whitchurch (Cardiff) & District Model Engineering Society had its headquarters was still British Rail property, and BR was always very keen to dispose of 'surplus' land, just as house-builders were itching to get their hands on it. So in 1984 the society had to vacate the site, lock, stock and tramway; Heath Junction was resited a quarter of a mile to the north,

and soon 45 houses swamped the entire site.

The new location for the miniature railway and tramway was at Heath Park, not far away and close to the edge of Heath Woods. Work began in 1985, but it was not until August 1987 that the new line could be opened to the public for the first time.

Felix Cunuder, C.Eng., MIEE, AM Inst. T, had come to Cardiff from Hastings Tramways (a trolleybus undertaking) in 1945. As engineer and rolling stock superintendent he had the task of changing over from tram to trolleybus operation. One of his notable achievements was to design a specially-light trolleyhead which weighed only 3½ pounds; these were adopted and quickly replaced all the original 8-pound heads. Mr Cunuder was also a very fine modelmaker and built three large-scale models of Cardiff trams, all of which were exhibited at the Welsh Industrial and Maritime Museum during 1983. These models were of No. 11, a 4-wheel open-top car, built in 1968; No. 44, a covered-top car built in 1969; and No. 50, a single-deck car built in 1971. The single-deck model was later displayed at the Tramway Museum at Crich, in Derbyshire.

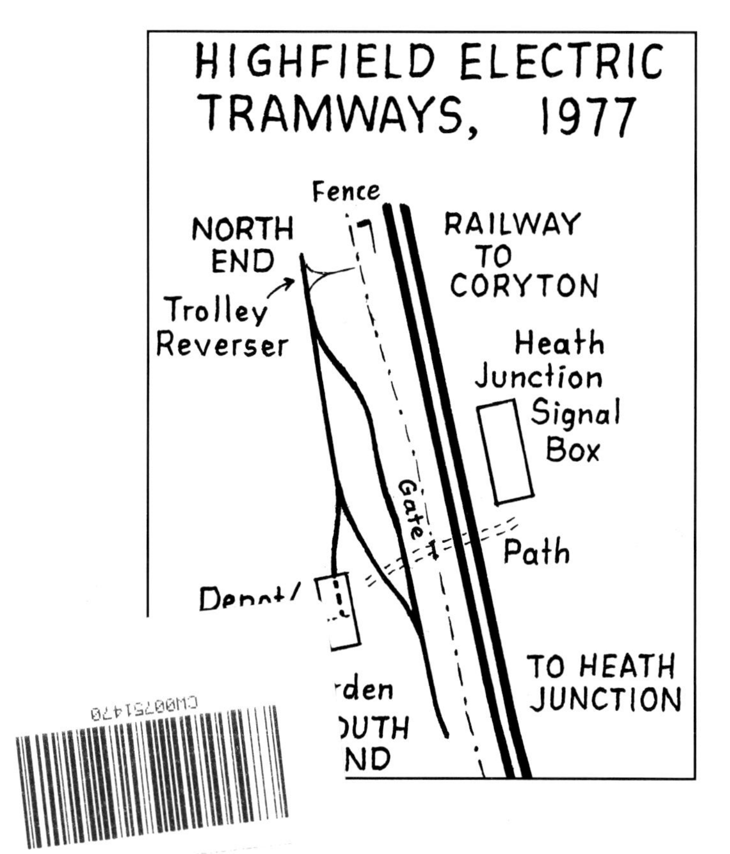